Community College Leaders on Workforce Development

Community College Leaders on Workforce Development

Opinions, Observations, and Future Directions

William J. Rothwell
Patrick E. Gerity
Vernon L. Carraway

AMERICAN
ASSOCIATION OF
COMMUNITY
COLLEGES

ROWMAN & LITTLEFIELD
Lanham • Boulder • New York • London

Published by Rowman & Littlefield
A wholly owned subsidiary of The Rowman & Littlefield Publishing Group, Inc.
4501 Forbes Boulevard, Suite 200, Lanham, Maryland 20706
www.rowman.com

Unit A, Whitacre Mews, 26-34 Stannary Street, London SE11 4AB

British Library Cataloguing in Publication Information Available

Library of Congress Cataloging-in-Publication Data Available

ISBN 9781475827415 (hardback : alk. paper) | ISBN 9781475827422 (pbk. : alk. paper) | ISBN 9781475827439 (electronic)

♾ ™ The paper used in this publication meets the minimum requirements of American National Standard for Information Sciences Permanence of Paper for Printed Library Materials, ANSI/NISO Z39.48-1992.

Printed in the United States of America

William J. Rothwell dedicates this book to his wife, Marcelina V. Rothwell; his son, Froilan Perucho; his daughter, Candice Szczesny; his grandsons, Aden and Gabriel; and his granddaughter, Freya.

Patrick E. Gerity dedicates this book to his wife, Cyn; his daughters, Rya, Jaissa, and Shayla; and to the leaders who dedicate their careers to community college workforce and economic development.

Vernon L. Carraway dedicates this book to his loving and supportive wife, Charlotte E. Watson Carraway; their children, Quincy, Langston, Leah, and Dorrian; and to all the students, from whom he has learned more than they will ever know.
A special acknowledgment is also extended to my son, Langston DuBois Lincoln Carraway; my mother, Mrs. Ruth E. McDaniel Carraway; my uncle, James E. McDaniel, D.D.S.; and his dear friend and devoted wife, Aunt Mamie V. Lawings McDaniel. Their direct and indirect contributions to the role to which I played in this book is immeasurable. I hope this final product will please them.

Contents

Preface

William J. Rothwell, Patrick E. Gerity, and Vernon L. Carraway

In the past seven years, U.S. community colleges have been recognized nationally by President Barack Obama and Vice President Joe Biden for the roles they play in educating millions of Americans for good paying jobs and for bolstering America's economic development. Thanks go to President Obama's cabinet members who have supported community college workforce and economic development initiatives—especially the Secretary of Labor, the Secretary of Education, and the Secretary of Commerce.

President Obama has met with community college presidents who contributed to this book. They include Dr. James Jacobs, President of Macomb Community College (Michigan), and Dr. Bryan Albrecht, President of Gateway Community and Technical College (Wisconsin), to discuss new federal workforce development programs for community colleges, such as the Trade Adjustment Assistance Community College Career Training Grant Program.

It is imperative to acknowledge the leaders at the American Association of Community Colleges (AACC), the primary advocacy organization for community colleges, who were responsible for making workforce and economic development a priority of America's community colleges. Specific recognition is owed to the current and past leadership at AACC, including Dr. George Boggs, Dr. Walter G. Bumphus, Kathy Mannes, Dr. James McKenney, Dr. David Pierce, and Jen Worth. AACC continues to stay on the cutting edge of workforce and economic development and to its credit has kept community colleges in America focused on supporting the growth of their local economies. The most valuable and specialized event related to this work is the annual AACC Workforce Development Institute.

The editors of this book—William Rothwell, Patrick Gerity, and Vernon Carraway—have recognized the critical need for preparing the new presidential leadership that will be emerging between now and 2018 when approximately 50 percent of the current community college presidents will be retiring. This book will be a guide for all community college presidents and others who recognize the value of community leadership in workforce and economic development. They will have the opportunity to hear from the best community college leaders on their successful experiences.

The interviews for this book were carried out between June 2015 and March 2016. All community college leaders were asked the same basic questions, and the chapters track these questions by theme:

- How would you define workforce development?
- What role do you believe your community college should play in workforce development?
- What role do you believe your community college should play in community development? Economic development? Individual career counseling? Training? Are there other roles community colleges should play in workforce development that they are not playing now?
- What barriers or challenges do you see community colleges facing in carrying out their roles now? In the future?
- Technology is changing the face of education. Many senior institutions are moving their curricula to online formats. How do you see technology affecting community colleges?
- What role should the community college President play in workforce development? Can you clarify what presidents should do and why you believe they should do that?
- What role should community college deans play in workforce development? Can you clarify what they should do and why you believe they should do that?
- What role should the community college faculty members play in workforce development? Can you clarify what faculty members should do and why you believe they should do that?
- What role should the community college workforce development leaders and staff play in workforce development? Can you clarify what workforce development staff members are doing well today? How could they improve?
- What can or should community leaders do to better support community colleges?
- What trends do you foresee in community colleges or the workforce that might affect the ability of community colleges to meet the needs of future students? Imagine visiting a community college 10 years from now. What would it look like? How would things be the same as or different than they are today?

- Imagine that you were having a conversation with business leaders from your community about the role of community colleges. What would you tell them about that role?

The interviewees did not have the benefit of seeing what their peers had to say. Thus, this book contains many independent views that also share common themes.

While other nations do not have the same community college framework as the U.S., the editors of this book believed it was important to add an international perspective. Two Thought Leaders from outside the U.S.—one from Germany and one from China—are included in part 3 of this book. They offer different, but nevertheless important, perspectives on locally positioned higher education.

Please see "About the Authors and Interviewees" for a complete list of our interviewees, their organizational affiliations, and background.

This book provides food for thought for years to come and will be a valuable resource for present and future community college leaders.

Acknowledgments

A project of this length and magnitude does not happen without the support of many people. Only three names grace the cover of this book, but several people took pride and felt ownership in it, ensuring that the project reached its full potential. Dr. P. Anthony Zeiss, President of Central Piedmont Community College, saw the worth of this project long before it took clear or final form. Jen Worth, Senior Vice President of Workforce and Economic Development at the American Association of Community Colleges, helped frame the piece and elevated new and bold voices in the field related to the topical areas of inquiry. To both of them, we say thank you.

Just as the development of community college executive leaders must be understood as a process embedded in an institutional context, so too must this work. We have been most fortunate over the course of this project to have interviewed a wide-ranging representation of a wonderful group of community college board executives and sitting presidents. We thank them all.

After full days of providing leadership within their own respective organizations, all made the sacrifice of time in support of this project. Perhaps the only consolation is that what we have learned may contribute to their generation's inheritance of a world better able to utilize an invaluable tool for that vulnerable time—"the transition into leadership."

Part I

Laying the Foundation

Part I lays the foundation for this book.

Chapter One

Common Themes in Community College Workforce Development

Community colleges in the U.S. are at a crossroads. Old leaders are retiring in record numbers, and new leaders are arriving. That situation creates both danger and opportunity. The opportunity is that new leaders can take a fresh look at the role of community colleges in workforce development, economic development, community development, training, and individual career counseling—among other issues. It is a danger because the lessons learned from the experience of seasoned leaders may be lost as experienced veteran leaders fade into retirement.

This book is intended to foster dialogue among Thought Leaders in community colleges about their role—and about the lessons they would like to pass on to future leaders. Most of the Thought Leaders interviewed for this book are community college presidents. In some cases, individuals are showcased that have unique vantages from which to make recommendations based on their deep and well-regarded workforce and economic development backgrounds. All have unique viewpoints worthy of presenting to future community college leaders.

Many people know that, over the next few years, many community college presidents will be eligible for retirement. This book addresses that reality by trying to capture some wisdom and institutional knowledge from those presidents. In the words of Gateway Technical College President and Chief Executive Bryan Albrecht of Kenosha, Wisconsin, "This is a terrific opportunity, and I am happy that you and your editorial staff are addressing this issue. I wish I had had something like this book to refer to when I started 10 years ago. I will read it, and I am sure that I will learn more about community colleges as I read it."

Consider this opening chapter as an executive summary of the book. Allow us to summarize common themes that emerged across the many Thought Leader interviews. "Given the large number of community college presidents, chancellors and/or CEOs that will transition from their roles in the coming years, we have a massive opportunity to inform the priorities of these new leaders. Economic resiliency and the workforce development strategies successful colleges have used to build robust economies warrants attention. This book shines light on many community college voices, and is to be commended for elevating the discussion." said Jen Worth, Senior Vice President, AACC.

DEFINING WORKFORCE DEVELOPMENT

All community college Thought Leaders agreed that workforce development is about helping people qualify for jobs and careers, maintain their skills in the face of changing business conditions, and prepare for future challenges such as promotions or technological change. Some Thought Leaders took narrower views of workforce development, but many opined that just about everything community colleges do ultimately contributes to developing the workforce.

THE COMMUNITY COLLEGE ROLE IN WORKFORCE DEVELOPMENT

All community college Thought Leaders agreed that community colleges play a critical role in workforce development. According to Clover Park Technical College Special Assistant to the President Mabel Edmonds of Lakewood, Washington:

> Workforce development leaders and staff are those closest to the workforce system and how it operates. Their primary role is to ensure the president/faculty/staff at their college stay abreast of workforce trends, needs, issues, funding sources, and best practices. Another role is to facilitate the planning, implementation, and assessment of the college's workforce development delivery system and outcomes. For the most part, workforce development leaders and staff are knowledgeable and do a good job. However, improvement is needed in providing the leadership necessary to have an effective workforce development system within colleges. Silos still exist; it's difficult to bring faculty and staff together to take stock, coordinate, and collaborate at a high level to achieve the desired outcomes.

THE COMMUNITY COLLEGE ROLE IN COMMUNITY DEVELOPMENT, ECONOMIC DEVELOPMENT, INDIVIDUAL CAREER COUNSELING, TRAINING, AND OTHER ISSUES

All community college Thought Leaders agreed that community colleges play important roles in community development, economic development, individual career counseling, training, and other issues. Many said that "workforce development *is* community development and economic development." Training is part of workforce development.

But workforce development is bigger. In the words of Gateway Technical College President and Chief Executive Bryan Albrecht:

> There are many roles community colleges can play. One is workforce development. But our role is bigger than that. In economic development, we look at our community colleges as bringing new resources to the community, state and federal grants allow us to leverage training capacity and adapt to changing talent needs. Product development is one area where we work closely with our local and regional businesses to leverage the capacity. Another strategy is business incubation and entrepreneurship: I think it's critical, and many community colleges are involved in developing opportunities for new businesses to flourish. We host a business incubator site, and we have faculty, students, and intellectual property readily available. We've developed what's called an accelerator program for small business start-ups. If a large company has a new product it wants to launch, we partner with them. If it's a small business trying to get off the ground, we develop funding mechanisms and align venture capitalists. And if it's a training issue, we try to align new services and bring in new, additional funds to support the training.

Individual career counseling services may stand improvement. As Arkansas Northeastern College President James Shemwell of Blytheville, Arkansas, said:

> We ought to do career counseling on the first day that students walk in the door. I formerly was Dean for Technical Programs here and the students, as part of their graduation process, would have to come by and see me. I would sign their graduation forms and verify that they had met the requirements and all of that. I can't tell you how often I would see just an ashen look on students' faces when I would ask them, "What are you going to do now? What does the future look like for you; what kind of job do you think you will get?" And they just had this look wash over them, and they would say, in a hundred ways, "I wish I knew at the beginning what I know now. I wouldn't have pursued this. I didn't know what the work environment was going to be like."
>
> That information is available. It is available up front. Since I became president, we changed admission standards. We also make sure that every student seeking a certificate or degree meets with one of three advisors their first semester and maybe during their first year if they are developmental. But

they meet with one of three advisors. We are a small institution. Last year we averaged about 1,400 students per semester, 1,400 to 1,500. We are down. We used to be about 2,000, but the economy has gotten better, so our numbers are down. But that is how we can get by with three people.

There is the Transfer Advisor; there is a Career and Technical Education Advisor; and there is an Allied Health Advisor. Depending on the students' initial area of interest, they will see one of those three people. They must fill out a short little form that asks questions about what they are interested in. It asks what does this pay and what the job growth prospects are for this. How a student could answer that is because they have someone there to facilitate and direct them to informative websites. The Department of Labor website is one place that contains this information.

CHALLENGES COMMUNITY COLLEGES FACE

Almost all community college Thought Leaders pointed to diminishing government funding as a major challenge that community colleges face. Beyond that, they pointed to a range of other challenges. Among them:

- Managing the issues imposed by geographical limitations
- Doing what we have always done
- Dealing with unfunded mandates
- Bringing programs up to scale
- Building and maintaining industry partnerships
- Handling equipment costs
- Dealing downstream with the aftereffects of social promotion in education
- Managing immigration issues
- Addressing issues associated with the fact that baby boomers are exiting the workforce but the baby bust generation is not entering in sufficient numbers to make up for the exits
- Acquiring adequate political clout
- Comparing the value of industry certification and degrees
- Keeping up with technological change
- Finding people who can communicate, and relate on an interpersonal level, with others
- Keeping an open-door policy
- Maintaining good relations with communities
- Keeping up with fast-paced changes in business and industry skill requirements
- Maintaining up-to-date skills among faculty members

HOW TECHNOLOGY AFFECTS COMMUNITY COLLEGES

All community college Thought Leaders saw technology as having an enormous impact on community colleges. Many agreed that online learning is changing education, though the Thought Leaders expressed reservations about relying on it as a total substitute for face-to-face classroom experiences. Several also pointed out that technology is changing the educational environment, affecting admissions, billing, and many other ways that colleges contact their communities and their regions. Some expressed concern that they face resistance from faculty who prefer classroom to online teaching.

THE ROLE OF THE COMMUNITY COLLEGE PRESIDENT IN WORKFORCE DEVELOPMENT

All community college Thought Leaders expressed the view that the President has a valuable role to play in workforce development. To carry out that role, presidents should be active in their communities to keep a finger on the pulse of those communities. In the words of Gateway Technical College President and Chief Executive Bryan Albrecht:

> The community college President must be the champion for our community. He or she helps to shape the vision of why the community college exists and what value it plays in workforce development strategy. By saying that, I mean he or she must spend time in the community to understand the community's needs. I serve on 60 boards. I am very active in the community, and I believe that helps me to take the community's pulse.
>
> However, not everything is driven by the workforce. I am on many community committees that allow me to do strategic planning and look at community development, foundation development, school district planning and development, and all those eventually will affect Gateway and workforce training. If the President does not remain active in community boards and committee work, he or she will find it hard to know all elements of what will make a community successful. People have their own unique priorities. My job is to connect those priorities with what Gateway can offer as services and become part of the solution for our community.
>
> We must emphasize that some students just want to sign up because they want to go to college. But we need to find out how Gateway can be a solution provider for our community. And that might well be workforce training, customization of that, or it might be workforce development or broadband initiatives within our community. And there are many ways we can become service providers. That may be a nontraditional view of the community college President role, but for me it's been something that I believe helps to create visibility for our campus. Even though we are 104 years old this year, many people have not heard about us or have not recently been on campus. We have a new

generation of community citizens who have gotten an impression of Gateway from one or two classes. But my job as President is to sell the entire Gateway package. The President connects community college resources to the community and must find more ways to build community connections.

THE ROLE OF COMMUNITY COLLEGE DEANS, FACULTY, AND WORKFORCE DEVELOPMENT STAFF IN WORKFORCE DEVELOPMENT

All community college Thought Leaders pointed to the important role played by deans, faculty, and the community college workforce development staff.

According to Macomb Community College President James Jacobs of Warren, Michigan:

> Community college deans, like other mid-level managers, can't just be administrative pencil pushers where they take Perkins Act money and fill out the right forms. They have to develop themselves as leaders and visionaries. Part of that is understanding the needs of their community, identifying what skill sets are necessary, and dealing with companies and their needs.
>
> Unfortunately, for many reasons which we don't have time to get into, most community college workforce deans tend not to do those things. They are more administrative and make sure that their desk is clean as opposed to seeing themselves more as leaders. The compliance aspect of the job gets overrated, and the visionary part of the job underrated. Unfortunately, scant attention in community college leadership programs is paid to this issue. There are two organizations—professional growth organizations—for community college deans, but the state of leadership and vision is not as high as it should be.

Faculty play the pivotal role. They are the face of the college to students, and many students remain in their communities and become community leaders. According to Bevill State Community College President Larry A. Ferguson of Sumiton, Alabama:

> With faculty we have to often convince them they need to be at the cutting edge of their fields. If they're not on the cutting edge, their students will not have a meaningful credential when they graduate. For many, we see and hear the reluctance until we get them into a session.
>
> We recently facilitated a two-week session at Toyota. We had instructors both from the secondary schools and from our colleges immersed in advanced manufacturing. They loved it. But at first many said they didn't want to give up two weeks of the summer for it. We compensate them. But even then we get resistance. But, ideally, once they are exposed to professional development, the energy is so intense they don't want to be left behind. They find out that they can't keep teaching industrial maintenance classes unless they know what new issues the instructors are talking about. I think it is a cultural thing.

Create a culture where learning is part of what adjunct and full-time faculty are expected to do. So we must build the right expectations. Most build that into the annual performance evaluation piece for faculty. We ask what they have done this year to ensure that they're on the cutting edge.

About workforce development staff, Bevill State Community College President Larry A. Ferguson also had this to say:

We went through a process several years ago where we redesigned all of the workforce development units of our 16 colleges. They were rebranded and were called Workforce Solutions. We also reexamined what those individuals should do.

One thing you have to be careful of is that often staff members will be given titles relating to workforce development but they haven't had adequate training to prepare them for that. To my knowledge, there is no major in that anywhere. Make sure they are adequately trained and that they are clear about what they should do and what results they should achieve.

Mission creep is a problem. That happens when we throw things at workforce development units because we do not know where else to assign them. Be very careful that the activities they are being assigned truly are linked to community, economic, and workforce development. I think it is a clarification of roles—an understanding of what is needed and not letting that department within the college just become a catchall.

I know you have probably seen that happen or heard talk of that. We must be concrete and precise. Front-line workforce development staff meets with clients, performs needs analysis, contracts for the training, and shepherds projects through to completion. We should give them short targeted goals—three to five—to guide their performance each year. It is not magic, but I think it is all about clarity of goals.

WHAT COMMUNITY LEADERS SHOULD DO TO SUPPORT COMMUNITY COLLEGES

Community college Thought Leaders felt that community leaders should be encouraged to say good things about the college and point to how it can contribute to community improvement. As Central Piedmont Community College President P. Anthony Zeiss of Charlotte, North Carolina, pointed out:

First community leaders need to be advocates for the college. They need to be advocates with policy makers and anyone else that they talk to.

When I first came to Charlotte, I had an experience with our economic development department at the Chamber of Commerce. The first day I got on this job, on December 1, 1972, I met a woman on the airplane. She was a site selector, and she told me she would go to Greensboro and Spartanburg but was flying into Charlotte. I asked, Why aren't you looking into Charlotte, because it is a better place to go. That statement astonished her. I gave her information and called the Chamber of Commerce. The Chamber attracted her company to Charlotte. I thought that experience would signal to economic developers I want to be a player with them.

It took about six years before I could convince them that one key incentive for relocating or new start-up plants is the ability to get and keep skilled workers. Since then, they have had us at the table. But it took a long time to convince the economic development people because they wanted to boast about the local university. And I finally had to come out and say, "Most of the jobs you are recruiting are not university graduate jobs."

The county supports our collaborative with 15 community colleges in a 29-county region in North and South Carolina and appreciates our collaborations with the public university. Students who want to transfer to the university go on as juniors.

TRENDS AFFECTING COMMUNITY COLLEGES

What does the future hold in store for community colleges? What trends will be most influential in shaping the future for community colleges and the workforce? Thought Leaders had much to say in answer to these questions, expressing views that community colleges will:

- Invest more in public–private partnerships
- Build more positive images
- Continue to face diminishing public funding support
- Experience increasing regulations, often as unfunded mandates
- Face more immigrants
- Face issues with facility safety
- Build even closer ties to businesses and the communities
- Consider offering baccalaureate degrees
- Pay attention to soft (interpersonal) and hard (technical) skills

FINAL WORDS

The present prospects and future trends affecting community colleges are bright. While there are challenges to be overcome, the opportunities outweigh the barriers.

Part II

Issues in Community College Workforce Development

Part II addresses the following issues:

- Defining workforce development
- The community college role in workforce development
- The community college role in community development, economic development, individual career counseling, and training
- Present and future barriers and challenges faced by community colleges in carrying out their roles
- How technology is changing the face of education
- The community college President's role in workforce development
- The community college Dean's role in workforce development
- The community college faculty member's role in workforce development
- The role of community college workforce development leaders and staff in workforce development
- What community leaders can do to support community colleges
- Trends affecting the ability of community colleges to meet needs of future students
- Conversations with business leaders about the role of community colleges

Chapter Two

Defining Workforce Development

Community college leaders were asked, "How would you define workforce development?" The question provides a baseline to determine how much thought the leaders have given to that issue. It is a fundamental starting point for what community college leaders think about the issue.

According to Kenosha, Wisconsin–based Gateway Technical College President and Chief Executive Bryan Albrecht, "Workforce development is such a broad term. Many people have multiple interpretations of what it means— including persons in our own community and industry. There are organizations called workforce development centers that support workforce development. In technical and community colleges, I define workforce development as aligning the training that's available through our community colleges with the skills that our employers are hiring for. So, if we can align the training with the skills being employed, then we are doing our due diligence in the workforce development issues of our times. And the needs change. That's what's so great about our community and technical colleges. Every year we have to be in touch with what those employer needs are and continually revive our workforce and development strategies."

A similar perspective was shared by others. According to Moorhead, West Virginia–based Eastern West Virginia Community and Technical College President Charles Terrell:

> Workforce development is the primary mission of a community college. Unfortunately, in the community college environment, we have typically separated academics from workforce development. I think they are both the same.
>
> Everything we do prepares our students to succeed in the workplace. Then other parts of our mission include community education, which is lifelong learning. But workforce development is our primary mission.

We are taking on an initiative here at Eastern—the concept of pre-kindergarten through a career. That provides a student with multiple pathways. In that initiative workforce development and short-term training could be one pathway.

I think when you define workforce development, it builds individual skills. It provides them with critical knowledge. Skill development includes hard-skills and soft-skills development for individuals to succeed in workplaces. Probably the most important thing is to help people compete in a global economy.

That would be my general introduction to how we would define workforce development. It is very comprehensive. I don't think we should narrow it down to training for business and industry or just short-term training only. Some people define workforce development as delivering commercial driver's license training. It is everything that we do at the community college.

Not only do we have a role to prepare people for the workplace, but we also have a part to play in preparing them to be good citizens. Many students at our community college want to acquire new skill sets to find new career pathways in a tough economy. It becomes a timing issue of how important it is for them to get back into the economy and to become self-sufficient.

Tempe, Arizona–based Rio Salado College President Chris Bustamante sees

workforce development as a partnership developed within a community of ecosystems. It's more local and regional because we are operating through colleges that serve residents of our communities. We engage our community and regional networks to gain a greater understanding in addressing the needs of workers and businesses. As a community college, we connect students to that network, and try to ensure that they have pathways to jobs, and that the training and education they receive is relevant to the workplace.

That is why people are talking more about competency-based education and creating relevancy between what students already know and the new knowledge that they need to acquire to earn a certificate or degree. That's really how I see it, connecting students and employers to educational programs that lead to successful pathways and workplace opportunities.

Kenosha, Wisconsin–based Gateway Technical College Vice President of Business and Workforce Solutions Deborah Davidson notes that

when defining workforce development, an understanding of the local context is vital. What does your local workforce look like? What are the industries in your area? What sectors are represented most in your area at the very top level? You have to dig deeper, sector by sector, and find out what are the needs of manufacturing; what are the needs in the financial service sector; what are the needs in the health care sector. Community college leaders must understand the environment in the geographic area they serve.

We continually ask what other programs or services we might offer to help better prepare our workforce. We know we can help workforce development through degree programs and credit-bearing programs, but we also know there are so many other ways that community colleges can positively impact workforce and economic development.

Solutions such as customized training, apprenticeships, or providing access to skill assessments that assist companies with hiring or employee development plans are among our offerings. Working with local career one-stops, economic development partners, faith-based organizations, and other community-based organizations helps us to better understand needs and trends from a variety of perspectives.

Our workforce partners help us uncover needs and then we come together to identify who is best prepared to fill those needs and the related skills gaps. We serve unemployed and underemployed individuals by upskilling them and providing education that allows individuals to reach the next level. We offer assessments and skill gap analysis as a starting point for individuals.

When we work with employers, we start with the end in mind and ask them to identify what they want the employee to know and be able to perform. They may, for instance, describe the end result as wanting skilled machine operators. How does an employer know what their people know? Do these workers understand safety? Blueprint reading? Math?

We look at what workers know, compare it to what they must know to perform, and then close the gaps. If we were to teach machine operation first, that may not improve the workers' skill level because they don't have the foundational knowledge on which to build. Individuals are not all coming at the topic from the same background or from the same level of understanding, so we assess and then target training to reach the desired learning outcomes. Employers understand that this will provide a better return on their training investment. They also understand that the assessment can be used as part of an employee's development plan.

According to Prestonsburg, Kentucky–based Big Sandy Community and Technical College President Devin Stephenson:

> I believe now, more than ever, workforce development is an essential component of community and economic development regardless of where a community college is located. Community colleges are even more critical now during the financial crisis we are experiencing in eastern Kentucky. We have major challenges here with the loss of jobs in the energy resource sector (primarily coal). Workforce development sits at the same table as the academic leadership and the financial leadership of our institution. Within three weeks of my arrival, I moved the workforce development leader of the college to the President's Cabinet level to emphasize the importance of our leadership in transforming the workforce of eastern Kentucky.
>
> To be honest, in the short time I have been here, I have spent more time in workforce development, with a direct connection to community and economic development, than with any other institution I have led. I have spent as much time building relationships externally for the purpose of enhancing our institution's capacity as I have internally because of the demand and challenges facing our region.

I would say that a good community college—a great community college—would approach workforce development as a top priority and create relevant programs and services that will transform its respective region. This is a key component from the perspective of sustainable economic security for both the individual and the region. That is where I think many community colleges get it wrong. They solely focus on the big picture and don't focus on how they develop individuals to build density.

Ultimately, we are looking at creating sustainable family wages for individuals in this region and our workforce development division is the primary vehicle making that happen by connecting individuals to their futures—bright futures. Our goal at Big Sandy Community and Technical College is to change this region one student, one opportunity at a time.

Also, I think effective workforce development is a collaborative effort with numerous partners in a region. An effective president will envision those partnerships and opportunities in all areas of the college, especially as they are applicable to external relations. Through workforce development we must focus on skills development and deployment that closes the skills gap so we create a region, especially in eastern Kentucky, that is more marketable and ready for a successful industrial recruiting effort and prepared to meet the demands of our contemporary economy and the global marketplace.

Here is a perfect example. Right now in eastern Kentucky we are about to install thousands of miles of dark fiber, and it is coming from a statewide broadband effort. Eastern Kentucky will benefit from the first phase of the project. We immediately recognized that there would be an immediate demand for technicians to splice and test the more than 3,000 miles of fiber. In my first week on the job, I met with our staff and leaders, including those in government (local, state, and federal) and the regional Workforce Investment Board, to discuss this challenge. It was important to bring the right people to the table that could create a quality, certifiable program and provide the support and financial services to train the unemployed and underemployed in our region. We did that.

Within a short period, we had faculty members certified through the Fiber Optic Association of America, and we launched that program on August 17. Since that time, we have filled classes, and now the demand for this fast-track training for high-speed jobs is serving students from more than 10 states.

When we talk about workforce development, we are not only talking about looking at the skills gap, but we are talking about being responsive, agile, transformational, relevant, and getting about the business of doing it without the red tape and bureaucracy that often plagues our higher education structures. People are seeking streamlined workforce training that leads to a job and a bright future.

The project was originally conceived through a consultant who had approached the University of Pikeville. President Paul Patton—who is the former Governor of the State of Kentucky and created the community college system in Kentucky—called me to say this effort was something that Big Sandy Community and Technical College should do and not the university.

Governor Patton invited me to a meeting where I joined representatives from the University of Pikeville, the City of Pikeville, AT&T, Appalachian Wireless, and Mountain Telephone. Also in attendance were funders from the

Economic Development Agency, the Department of Commerce, and the Workforce Investment Board. Governor Patton asked me to share what our college could do for the program, and I simply spoke from my heart about workforce development and its importance in transforming eastern Kentucky.

At the conclusion of the meeting, he asked for a proposal. Not only did we develop the program, but also the grant funders are providing $3.2 million to us to construct a new advanced technology center on our Pikeville campus. Our college has guaranteed the match of $1.2 million, and so we will build a $4.5 million facility in Pikeville to provide state-of-the-art fiber optics training and future advanced technology education, the first of its kind in Kentucky.

The vision became a reality because we appropriately and deliberately collaborated. A community college cannot operate on an island. It must be externally focused on the demands and stresses of the external environment and proactively respond with ways in which the college can play a role in solving problems and delivering solutions. A leader today, to be effective in a president's role, must be visibly engaged in making a difference or else the college will not be successful in community, economic, and workforce development efforts.

According to Warren, Michigan–based Macomb Community College President James Jacobs:

"Workforce development" is a term which refers to the production and expansion of the talent capacity of a community. It is bounded by what an economic region does in the important sectors with skills needed for that region to advance. It is very much connected to economic development. The reason I want to make these distinctions is that the relationship between workforce development and economic development is critical to what community colleges should do.

That leads to the second question, which is the role. Community colleges must change their roles. In the past, community colleges have been primary institutions which react to community demands for certain skill sets and talent. Typically, that means community colleges respond to company needs for their employees. While that still is an important function, an additional function is that community colleges must try to determine what future needs will exist. Preparing the future workforce will become a significant workforce development role for community colleges.

Let me be specific about what I mean. Let me use the example I am most familiar with because it affects my community college. We are in an area where the automobile industry is the principal sector of employment, so we take seriously what goes on in the automobile industry. The high demand in the automobile industry is for welding. Welders and people who learn the skills of welding can get jobs. While that is a splendid thing, we also know by studying the industry that in the next 10 years the automobile industry will make products out of aluminum and other composites such as plastics and ceramics.

That means welders will still be needed. But demand will not be as high for them as in the past. Demand will shift to people who know chemistry, plastics, and know how to join composites. These skills are in short supply. What we have to do—and this is most difficult for a community college—is not just look at the present but try to make certain bets on what we see the future holding for our community and our employers.

Now, obviously, there is risk in this. Sometimes mistakes will be made. You can't plan effectively in all cases, but a good community college studies its community and tries not just to understand what exists now and react to it but to anticipate emerging needs. That will mean the difference between a successful community college and others.

According to Harrisburg, Pennsylvania–based Harrisburg Area Community College President John J. Sygielski:

> Workforce development is an approach to enhance a region's economic stability and the prosperity of the people by focusing on people rather than on business. Workforce development is a human resource strategy. We take a holistic approach to overcome the barriers faced by a region and identify what the area needs at present and in the future. How do we translate those needs into training and education in high schools, workplaces, and community colleges?
>
> Career pathways is the work we are doing in high schools and in the community college. In high schools, we are trying to understand the school curriculum and where we can more closely align a better two-plus-two-plus-two curriculum with higher education. In community colleges, we try to make sure students, high school counselors, and business community representatives create understanding of what needs to be taught from the 11th grade through the associate and/or baccalaureate degrees. A baccalaureate degree is not always necessary because a certificate could be what the business community needs.
>
> The work we do regarding a high school's pathway program is to expose high school students to career pathways and help them understand what careers exist and what kind of training and education they need to gain entry into those careers. For the underemployed and unemployed, we work with the Pennsylvania CareerLink. Pennsylvania CareerLink is a collaborative project between multiple agencies to provide career services to Pennsylvania employers, potential employees, and others to understand underemployed and unemployed issues so we can tailor workforce training and education training to their needs in our region.

Palatine, Illinois–based William Rainey Harper College President Ken Ender thinks that

> workforce development could be described both as a program at a community college and as a goal. It could mean both a noun and a verb. You could also define it from the goal perspective, mostly within the context of a regional or a community institutional or an economic development initiative in the community college space. It has both knowledge and skills competency transmission elements that affect the work that the community college might do. It might

also represent a sector, industry, or company from a goal perspective that a region or community is trying to place in their location. That's where it gets into economic development.

The daily workforce development of a community college centers on the transmission of skills, knowledge, and competencies that have labor-value attached to them. Underneath that comes the foundation of that work, the more general education competencies we associate with liberal arts education. Regarding skills and knowledge is the transmission of the capacity to think critically, solve problems, and work in diverse environments, have appropriate interpersonal skills and numerical literacy, and demonstrate technology skills that will support whatever work individuals are doing.

Supporting a similar view, Sumiton, Alabama–based Bevill State Community College President Larry A. Ferguson notes:

There was a time when people would separate workforce development from economic development. I heard a speaker say that workforce development and economic development are essentially the same thing. The reason is that a national magazine has indicated, in an annual poll, that the number-one business need centers on the workforce.

For companies to expand or grow, or to entice them to move into a state, the first question will always be about the local workforce. Any business needs a highly skilled and competent workforce. That concern has evolved, and we now hear about the need for a "highly technical workforce." For me, workforce development means providing our employer base throughout the multiple sectors we serve with a competent, highly skilled workforce to meet the needs or demands of their particular industry.

I will give you an example. We heard several months ago that our Ford plant would take the F-150 truck and make it out of aluminum. I immediately wondered, when I read that story in *MotorWeek*, from where they would get high-grade aluminum. We immediately recognized that was an economic opportunity. So our cabinet for economic development worked with our aluminum providers in the state to take a proactive position, create curriculum around metallurgy and material science, and have these ready so we literally could get the presidents of two of our colleges—one being Owensboro and the other being Bowling Green, which is Southcentral Community and Technical College—to sign a support letter that, "yes, if you bring these companies in we are ready to go to train your workforce."

That example illustrates how we have to be attuned to all things happening from an economic perspective. We must be in tune with our business and industry partners, which we have always known we had to do, but we must go beyond that to develop a hypersense to be proactive to anticipate what will happen or what will be needed. Those colleges are very dynamic; they worked quickly. But we had no curriculum and no programs in the state around metallurgy or material sciences.

Another thing I will say about workforce development. I heard an English professor ask, "What does what I do have anything to do with workforce development?" Ultimately students come to the community college either for a credential like a certificate, a degree, or to transfer to a university to earn a baccalaureate or doctorate degree. But wherever students go, they end up in the workforce. Every point of contact they have along their education continuum prepares them for the workforce.

Brooklyn Park, Minnesota–based Hennepin Technical College President Merrell Irving observes:

When we break the phrase "workforce development" down into two separate parts, it defines itself. The *workforce* comprises individuals engaged in or available for work, including individuals anticipating entering the workforce, currently in the workforce, and looking to be promoted within the workforce. These are the three top components of the workforce. When *developing* the workforce, we are preparing workers with needed skills through education, training, and development to address the hiring demands of employers and to place workers in positions with career advancement opportunities.

The three major workforce groups are individuals entering, individuals maintaining positions, and individuals looking to be promoted within an organization. As we create academic and lifelong learning programs, we must remain focused on those three groups.

One example of individuals anticipating entering the workforce are our community and technical college students whom we are educating through traditional pathways, whether they are passing through a high school program, linked to a two-year community or technical college certificate or degree program, or through a four-year university. Another example is those who are in applied learning programs through apprenticeships wrapped within academic programs or apprenticeships in association with industries that directly train individuals.

Examples of the latter can be seen in some other countries, such as Germany, where apprenticeship programs start early on and often include both an educational and on-the-job component. In the U.S., we begin many apprenticeship programs within the latter part of a higher education experience.

But getting back to the subject at hand: developing and providing programs for those that enter the workplace through traditional pathways, nontraditional workers entering the workforce, and workers anticipating entering the workforce, including those who have been laid off. We must address the needs for such persons. We must close the skills gap by equipping individuals with the knowledge, skills, and experience required for available jobs.

The inability to attract and retain a skilled workforce is intensified as organizations find themselves simultaneously managing the four generations of workers. One group comprises baby boomers who, because of the Great Recession, lost substantial retirement savings and now find themselves having to work longer than they planned. In addition, many baby boomers continue to work at least part-time in retirement. This is historically unheard of in the U.S. How does a community or technical college prepare the present workforce to become, and remain, competitive? We have to plan strategically for those who enter, remain, and exit the workforce. That is the delicate condition in which we find the U.S. workforce today.

According to Charlotte, North Carolina–based Central Piedmont Community College President P. Anthony Zeiss, "Workforce development is human development, and it shouldn't matter where or how people learn. For example, we have many veterans returning to our college. They have military occupational specialties that may align with university or community college curricula. Workforce development is any set of activities and resources that the military has provided to assist these veterans to achieve their career objectives and prepare them for jobs as civilians."

According to Washington, D.C.–based American Association of Community Colleges Senior Vice President Jen Worth:

> I see workforce development as a process that occurs in concert with industry partners and economic development professionals, in which individuals are provided with the knowledge and skills necessary to seek or retain meaningful employment. Workforce development must be rooted in training and education that is both relevant and based on arising, and not just the current needed skills. While workforce development is clearly about preparing individuals, it cannot be discussed without also talking about economic development.
>
> When we talk about workforce development and economic development together, we are taking a more holistic approach that takes into account the economic climate and demographics of the place in which the work is occurring. We align national and local partners in the higher education industry with federal, foundation, and national networks to ensure that lasting connections are forged with AACC members. We want those connections to occur at the leadership level (that is, presidents and chancellors), and we want to ensure that we are disseminating best practices to infuse into the daily activities of workforce development deans and programs.

Cleveland, Ohio–based Cuyahoga Community College Executive Vice President of Workforce, Community, and Economic Development William Gary regards "workforce development as the preparation of a qualified pipeline of workers to meet the workplace and workforce demands of business and industry":

> First of all, we must understand what those demands are and the industry sectors that are driving the local and regional economy. We must meet with the CEOs of industries to determine their particular wants and wishes and couple that with not only the educational components but with community-based organizations that can help partner and contribute to identifying potential students to move into community college workforce development programs. It's also important to align that with the economic development, community, and business interests so that everyone is on the same page regarding a regional workforce development strategy.
>
> We work in close partnership with several community-based organizations to include local school systems (for example, the Cleveland Metropolitan School District); serve on local Workforce Development Boards/Economic

Development Authorities in the Northeast Ohio area. We have aligned ourselves with the local and regional philanthropic organizations to contribute to
social, economic, and educational projects. We are now working with all of
those to collaborate on developing a unified strategic plan for workforce development, with the community colleges at the forefront.

Lakewood, Washington–based Clover Park Technical College Special
Assistant to the President Mabel Edmonds offers a succinct definition:
"Workforce development is the comprehensive approach/system that includes education, training, and services to prepare individuals for career
pathways and employment opportunities, as part of the global economy."

Blytheville, Arkansas–based Northeastern College President James
Shemwell says:

> Workforce development provides skills-based training. That would include
> application-oriented practice in which individuals in groups prepare for careers
> in demand. The key words are *in demand*. I see that as a crucial opportunity; it
> is also a critical problem in the community college ranks across the country.
> Are we preparing people for careers in demand? That is what we should do.
>
> Workforce development can have a narrow or broad definition. We usually
> think about "workforce development" with a narrow definition. I think about
> three delivery methods. We traditionally think of open-enrollment offerings,
> postsecondary programs. We also think of certificate programs and degree
> programs that, upon completion, prepare students to go into a field at some
> level and be able to vie for jobs and have acceptable careers. That is one
> delivery method and is the traditional view.
>
> Customized training for one or several employers is the second one. Most
> community colleges do that. For us, that has become a real niche. We started
> something we called the Solutions Group about 20 years ago. We named it
> that. The day we named it, I drew the logo which we use today. I cut my teeth
> in workforce education here at Arkansas Northeastern College. It is not true to
> say that was my first job. My first job was as an off-campus coordinator here
> for one of our satellite campuses. But a line item in my job description said
> that we needed a vehicle for workforce education—for workforce develop-
> ment.
>
> The Solutions Group comprised faculty members we hire to do customized
> training. The traditional model that existed for us—and I think for many insti-
> tutions—is that, if we train for business and industry, we will find adjuncts to
> do that. If our faculty has the right skill set and inclination, we might use some.
> But they will do that on the side.
>
> Instead, we found instructors with experience in business and industry and
> in the discipline they would teach—whether we hired former plant managers,
> electrical engineers, or mechanical engineers—people like that. We want peo-
> ple with experience in that field. We also look for people as well with some
> academic credentials, but we were not fixated on that. We didn't insist on a
> master's degree. People think of that as the coin of the realm in community
> colleges—a master's degree—but that is true for transfer and not so much for

technical programs. What we look for are people who have licensure or some experience.

We have been very fortunate over the years. Mostly we found people with both academic credentials and industry background. We hired these workers, and I'd say they exclusively teach customized training. Occasionally they might teach a traditional class if it looks like their semester teaching load will be light; we might slot them in a traditional class to help move them closer to their full teaching load. But we do little of that because we want them to be available to train and teach at any time and at any place.

With companies we try to be flexible regarding our delivery. For instance, we have done classes at 2 a.m.; and we have done classes on a rotating schedule. We won a national award in 2005 because we delivered a two-year degree and partnered with a university nearby, delivering a four-year degree in partnership with them and offering the classes every eighth day. We did that because of the steel industry here.

People were four days on shift, four off. It was virtually impossible for them to take classes. That was before the onset of online education. But there are still classes that don't lend themselves that well to online, and so you still have the issue. We catch workers on their second day off. If class this week is on Tuesday, next week it will be on Wednesday, and the week after it is on Thursday. It rolls. It is important to have flexible delivery.

We price by the hour and not by the person, which is a radical idea. If a company wants—let's say they want training, supervisory training, or computer numeric control training, whatever, and they don't have 10 people that need this. They don't have enough to "make a class." But they have three people, and they would be glad to pay for this, top dollar, because if they can't find a solution locally, they will have to fly these people somewhere, put them up in a hotel, and pay a private vendor an expensive fee to do that.

For customized training, we charge by the hour. Companies decide how cost-effective they would like to make it. They can send one person, or they can send 21 persons—that's up to them. And do you know what? The model works. Companies will pay for it because it is a better economic value for them. We don't end up with this inability to deliver what is needed in the workplace because we can't "make a class" because we can't get enough people together.

We need to think outside the box on tuition, class size, and other issues. Let's just figure out how to make it work. If a company pays for the time, we bill by the instructional hour. We don't bill for preparation. We just bill for the time somebody is teaching. We can charge $150 per hour. They are glad to pay it. For us, it works.

Another thing we do is to custom-design solutions. The employer is facing an issue. Sometimes community college people think, "Let's see, let's find something canned that we have done before or some college class and inflict that on you." That is not our approach. We find out what the employer's problem is and then customize training exactly to solve that problem. If the training is worthy of credit and the employer would like their workers to receive credit, we see if we can do that. If not, who cares? The bottom line is we are trying to solve an issue, trying to meet a company's training need.

What we need to do is we have to build full-time capacity for workforce education and rely less on adjunct capacity. Adjunct instructors almost always—not always, but almost always—have other jobs. That is why we desire these people, because they are in some field in demand, and they are good at it. Those are the people you would want to put in front of a customer or employer—someone part of your college. You want to get those people. If they have jobs, then right away we are limited in delivery schedule because their first obligation must be to their employers.

We have restricted ourselves to nights, weekends, or online. We have to build full-time capacity and not look at workforce education as an offshoot or hybrid. I have seen that evolve in my time at the college.

Our college is 40 years old. We started with general education in the way I think most community colleges do. The associate was the first degree we had. That was what we were built around, the associate in arts, and then the college added career-type programs like associate in applied science programs. In several years, the college considered certificates—something less than two years. Then, in 2003, our college had a unique opportunity and experience.

We merged with a technical institute. Then we pulled in many technical programs, and it caused us to think in different ways. The transition I am talking about is one where we think in traditional academic terms of what college is. Workforce development is something we do besides that. That's something new we are doing; that is something extra we are doing.

We are reaching the realization that everything we do is workforce development at some level. It is workforce development if we are training people; it is workforce development if we are teaching people in our AA degree and they transfer to a university. When they major in something at that university, I would put it to you that 99 out of 100 are looking at something in hopes they will find a job when done. Maybe it is something they are just doing for laughs, but the other 99 are doing it for a career.

That irritates people who spent their lives in academia. But you know what, that is workforce development. It is all workforce development. We need to see it that way. We need to think past those traditional academic paradigms. We envision workforce development because we think exclusively regarding open offerings, degree and certificate programs, and we need to think more about customized training. We also need to think more about the three delivery methods.

The third delivery method is concurrent credit in high schools. We have a secondary center. Are those popular in Pennsylvania? Are you familiar with the concept?

That is relatively new for us. We have operated one for about 10 years. We are doing six career-type programs in our local high schools. They bus the students into one of our campuses, and we do six programs. We have some that are traditionally male programs and some that are traditionally female. That is the other delivery method. We have to reach students earlier.

One challenge that colleges always face is trying to get young people to matriculate from high school to college. I think we are all doing a better job of that. We are doing a better job at ANC, but we still don't get the majority—or, at least, we don't attract them to Mississippi County, Arkansas. I know there are places around the country that probably have the majority of their students that go, but our college-going rate right here in the Mississippi Delta is less than 50 percent. What do we do about that?

One thing we do about that is we reach these students while they are still in high school and provide the training right there. What we have seen with that over the last 10 years, though, is there must be more than just this secondary center. We have seen our county's high-school-graduate college-going rate go up 10 percent over the last 10 years. We have reached 50 percent for probably the first time in our history. A big key in that is trying to reach students while they are still in high school.

Chapter Three

The Community College Role in Workforce Development

We asked Thought Leaders what role they believed community colleges play in workforce development. It was a natural next question beyond the request to define workforce development. Their views demonstrated a comprehensive sense of that role.

According to Kenosha, Wisconsin–based Gateway Technical College President and Chief Executive Bryan Albrecht, "I believe that the role of the community college in workforce development is pivotal. The history of community colleges is grounded in supporting the workforce of a local or regional economy. That's why, in Wisconsin, we have 16 technical colleges broken up by regional and geographical boundaries of counties. And it's similar in other states. There are about 1,200 community colleges across the country where nearly every citizen has access to higher education on a community basis, which means we really train for a local or regional workforce. Again, I think the community college role in regional development is pivotal to building strong communities. And it has been a part of our mission at Gateway since 1911."

That view was supported by Brooklyn Park, Minnesota–based Hennepin Technical College President Merrell Irving:

> Community and technical colleges must work with local and regional business industries to identify internal and external needs and opportunities. Workforce development involves transforming employees to become flexible to adapt to changes within the organization. Internally, educators look at the organization's quality improvement needs and the types of training and education current employees need in order for the organization to remain competitive.

Educators must also assess potential employees in order to help employers identify the right people for the right jobs. Community and technical colleges must provide potential workers with the skills to complete tasks needed by employers to allow the organization to remain competitive in the global marketplace.

In order for educators to know what those skills are, they must target specific industries or clusters of occupations and work to develop an extensive understanding of the industry dynamics and workforce needs. The job of community and technical colleges is to understand what is needed in specific industries. Workforce development educational leaders assess the potential employee, provide the necessary skill development and training to the potential employee, and then provide this individual to the organization. But it does not stop there. Organizations need ongoing training and career programs that continuously strengthen the skills and abilities of their employees and create an environment that supports, motivates, and provides opportunities for employees to develop to their full potential.

The community and technical colleges are the economic engine for local and regional municipalities and the state. Most individuals that come to a community or technical college are from the local area. They will most likely remain employed within the local area and state. Community and technical colleges have a direct economic impact on regional economies. Community and technical colleges have the most direct relationship with employers and offer opportunities for lifelong learning.

While most four-year universities pride themselves on research, community and technical colleges provide a mix of theory and application, and are influenced by local employers, who sit on the advisory boards for the college and act in tandem with the colleges to identify and meet local workforce needs. Who are we in competition with, and what should we provide? What do we need as workforce developers to meet employer needs now? Community and technical colleges can answer these questions better than any other local or regional institution.

Harrisburg, Pennsylvania–based Harrisburg Area Community College President John J. Sygielski adds to that view: "In addition to my engagement on the boards of regional chamber and economic development organizations, HACC's Associate Provost for Workforce Development and his team are working with the local and regional business community every day to identify what their needs are both internally and externally. Internally, they may look at their quality improvement needs and what kind of education and training current employees need to preserve the competitive stance of each business. Externally, we assess potential employees. We use American College Testing's [ACT] Work Keys, various skill assessments, and training products to help employers identify the right people to provide to employers so those employers can fill job vacancies with qualified people."

The central role of community colleges in local workforce development is reinforced by Charlotte, North Carolina–based Central Piedmont Community College President P. Anthony Zeiss:

One way to think of the community college's role is that we need an economic vision for our institution, our city, and our region to ensure jobs and future prosperity. We have had economic developers working hard and competing from city to city, trying to get jobs in the area. But there was no coordinated strategy. Worse, there was no vision. You know the Good Book says that the people without a vision perish.

I decided that we needed a vision. "You've got to have the vision to get where you wish to be—whether you're an individual, a community, a state, or a nation." A former Superior Court Judge, Chase Saunders, and I visited with various community leaders, and we developed a grassroots effort to launch an economic vision. That vision was to become a global hub of commerce. Now we have put that together. Five years later, we have made tremendous progress in boosting our competitive assets, and that has been one of the most rewarding things I have ever done. It finally dawned on me that if my friend and I didn't do it, who would do it?

The model for getting things done 15 years ago was for three or four of the most prominent, prestigious business leaders to decide where the community would go. Then everybody would follow. That was efficient. But that approach doesn't work anymore. Now people want to be more involved. We have a Global Vision Leaders Group, made up of 185 top business leaders throughout a 29-county region. Then we have 15 community college presidents that make up a community college collaborative group to make sure that skilled workers are available as we collectively move into a global economy.

This collaborative is important for two reasons. First, if we can't get the skilled workers for manufacturing, exporting, and intermodal transportation, then a vision is useless. That is why these community colleges are crucial, because they cater to middle-class jobs. That's what community colleges do well—prepare people for middle-class jobs. The second reason is that we need a nonpolitical entity helping this Global Vision Leaders Group to implement its comprehensive strategic plan. Once you politicize a community movement, you get opposition. A house divided cannot stand.

Effective community colleges like Central Piedmont Community College are proactive. We are not reactive. We always think ahead to anticipate what will happen. We often lead our community and our region toward a more definable future rather than merely reacting to problems as they arise. We have the power to convene people to set community goals.

The role of the community college is critical because no one else is embracing these global issues! We had a committee of leaders study "Charlotte Economic Development," which recommended a coordinated, strategic plan for Charlotte. The committee mentioned globalization throughout its recommendations. The Chamber and the Charlotte Regional Partnership agreed that they needed to develop a strategic plan because they didn't have one and they needed to demonstrate that we are involved in this global economic movement.

Much is happening now. We invited the U.S. Department of Commerce to teach our small and midsize businesses how to export. They have been doing that for about five years now through Central Piedmont Community College. Now the Charlotte region has been named the fastest-growing export region in the nation. A year ago, *Site Selection* magazine named us the seventh-largest global metropolitan region in America. That has not happened overnight, but it's been developed over the past five years.

Several other wonderful things have occurred. There was also a study done by IBM to determine the top 100 global metropolitan areas in the world, and our region was ranked around #35. We were also named the seventh-best foreign direct investment region in America.

We are astonished these things are happening! However, I suppose we shouldn't be surprised because we've worked hard at it. And we have put the Global Vision Leaders Group together. We hosted a German delegation to visit a recent Global Vision Leaders Group meeting. They were amazed and invited us to revisit their country. They want to adopt our model of how to become more global for their Rhine River Valley region.

According to Sumiton, Alabama–based Bevill State Community College President Larry A. Ferguson:

The Kentucky Community and Technical College System (KCTCS) is statutorily required to be the leader in workforce development and training. This year we worked with 5,000 companies. Some companies need workers with baccalaureate degrees and above. But many, as we know from multiple studies, just need certifications that require two years or less. Our role is to meet those workforce needs in efficient and effective ways.

Let me give you another example. In my state, as is true nationally, there is a shortage of individuals with a commercial driver's license (CDL). Interstate trucking jobs pay well. We are partnering with the Kentucky Trucking Association to help meet these needs. How do we better train people beyond just giving them a CDL? These carriers are turning away work every day because they don't have qualified professional commercial drivers to handle the jobs. They are in-state jobs; these are not jobs where they spend all their time on the road. They go home at night. We are being asked to do more strategic work even at that level that is more aligned with what the workforce of that sector must have to ensure that individuals can succeed.

Blytheville–based Arkansas Northeastern College President James Shemwell adds another perspective:

We must think of preparing students for success instead of failure. Sounds rather like a cliché. Let me specify. What I mean by that is that we established for the first time at ANC some admission standards. Before, basically, if you had the GED or diploma, it was an open door.

We did a study I was directly involved with about four years ago—before I became President. We looked at five years' worth of data. We defined student success as people who passed their classes or else made C or better in the developmental class. That was what they needed to move on in a remedial or developmental course. We correlated student success with either their ACT, Compass score, or Asset test score. We cross-walked those things and discovered those students who scored below a 15 on the ACT—which roughly correlates to about ninth-grade functional level—had an 11 percent chance of getting through English composition and a 3 percent chance of getting through college algebra. That result comes from five years of data.

Analyzing data is better than responding to anecdotal evidence. Anecdotal evidence depends on the latest anecdote you have heard. The best investment, one of the best investments that a community college can make, is data mining software. We must analyze data and stop relying solely on anecdotes. We did that, and what we discovered was shocking.

We set an admission standard, and it is multi-level. We said that for students who score less than a 15 on the ACT or a Compass equivalent, we will limit the range of programs to which they can immediately declare. What I mean by that is we've got a free service called Skills Tutor. Students can brush up on their skills. There is a facilitator to help them. They are not by themselves. They can brush up. It is not like the students can never declare these degrees, but they have to prepare for success. They will have to get their skills up so they can succeed in these programs.

Now, we have some other programs over here, though, and they are technical certificates or certificates of proficiency where our data shows that the success rates are not 11 percent and 3 percent. They start at 55 percent and go to 85 percent. Why I think that is—I can't prove this; we haven't done that study to prove it—but what common sense tells me is these certificate programs have better success rates because, with math and with grammar, the way I like to think of it is they are teaching vertically what the student must know.

What do I mean by that? We traditionally have taught those subjects horizontally. When we think about developmental education, here is where you tested, at the lowest level. Let's teach everything at the lowest level. When we are done with this semester, let's go to level 2 and teach everything at level 2 and then we are almost ready, so let's teach everything at level 3. At this point, they have probably been enrolled a year and a half.

What they do in these certificate programs is they say, Here are the things out of level 1 students must know. And let's get these things out of level 2, and there are even a few things in level 3—let's take those. And we are doing this to teach students—just what students must know for this discipline. It works. Students can get their minds around that. We said if students are below the 15, then they can declare these certificates like any other student could.

If students are below 11, we are talking about a sixth-grade functional level. If that is where we are, we need to go to adult education first, and we need to do intensive work to get skills up because students are not ready to succeed yet. We have to do that. We have to prepare students for success.

At ANC if we don't prepare these students for success, if we just let them come on in even if they are not ready, they are ripe to fail. I used to be one of these right-to-fail people. I'll confess. People have a right to fail. We ought to let them enroll and do what they think they can do. If they come in, and they fail, well, that chance has gone by. Maybe after a time, they could reapply and be eligible again, or maybe their life circumstances changed and perhaps economically they can afford to pay for college. For so many people that may not be the case, or they become so discouraged from that first experience they never come back. We are doing such a big disservice if we don't prepare people to succeed in college.

My VP for Community Relations says—and this is one of my favorite things I have heard—she hears people say that college is not for everybody. She says Arkansas Northeastern College *is* for everybody. Even if students are at this level with their skills, academically, that students are not ready to succeed, we have a pathway for them. We will work with students. It is for everybody. We may not all start at the same place, but that's acceptable. We want students to finish at the same place.

We have to do a better job of preparing these students for success instead of failure. The door is still open, but maybe not every program is on the first floor. There might be a few stairs to climb, but that is acceptable. We have a roadmap on how to get there, and we will exercise students and get them ready to climb those stairs.

I have to tell you when you ask me about workforce development, it is like punching 10 buttons on the jukebox. The jukebox will play for a while.

Prestonsburg, Kentucky–based Big Sandy Community and Technical College President Devin Stephenson gave his perspective on the role of community colleges by relating a personal experience:

I began my career at a small technical college in Alabama affiliated with the mining industry. During the early years of my administrative experience I saw firsthand the importance of being relevant to business and industry. Our institution had the only Alabama coal-mining academy and we delivered training for new miners, recertification training for currently employed miners, and safety training and response services to small mine operators who could not afford their own services. So from the beginning I understood how vital our higher education sector is to keeping the economy strong.

Primarily, I think community and technical colleges must be an active player in economic and community development, too, but workforce development is the most important piece of our work right now. Community colleges sit at the nexus of academia, industry, and local government. Think about it. We are positioned in the center, and when a big opportunity presents itself, the community turns to the community/technical college to make things happen. We are responsive and agile. That enables us to play a significant role not only in college preparedness but also in training the workforce to meet the needs of an ever-changing, global economy.

Also, I believe we are the sector of higher education to play that role. We can respond to the needs of the communities we serve because we are driven to respond and we are truly engaged in the communities we serve. Community and technical colleges have never been as important as they are now. It shows from the increased recognition we are receiving from all levels of government, as well as business and industry, and from our many successes in providing seamless pathways through education to jobs.

I believe we are viewed today as an essential, if not the most important, resource in addressing workforce development needs. Ultimately, because of our important position in communities throughout this nation, our role should be defined as central to every initiative that improves the quality of life for our citizens. As a president, I must not only lead but lead by example on how we improve the quality of life. That is a major focus of workforce for us here. We have a powerful and engaged workforce solutions program that generates significant revenue for our college but is also instrumental in transforming this region one student, one opportunity at a time. It is working!

Supporting Stephenson's view, Moorhead–based Eastern West Virginia Community and Technical College President Charles Terrell noted that community colleges

play the primary role in providing the nation with a skilled workforce and are closer to the grassroots in providing a skilled workforce to our community and region. That way our region can compete on a national level and also sometimes on a global scale.

When I first entered the workforce, and I can't remember the person who shared this with me, but it stuck with me for the last 10 or 15 years. Workforce development at the community college is like the front porch of a community college. Because many students see a community college as higher education, they hesitate about approaching us and asking questions. To reach them we must build their self-confidence.

When workforce development can engage with individuals in short-term training, it may develop self-confidence and build a relationship between the college and the individual. By building that relationship, it then provides the individual with greater awareness of other opportunities that the college offers. For the people that may go into the CDL four-week training program here at Eastern, we talk about entrepreneurship and how they can acquire additional skills to work on their own without going to a company.

I think that is the role of a community college: to build relationships. That is the key word—*community*. Workforce development can establish that sense of community for individuals. By building relationships, community colleges open the door on the front porch to come in to see the certificates, degrees, or industry certifications that are available. I think if individuals have that experience and they build their confidence, that will establish a lifelong relationship.

Many students in a community college, when they complete whatever training or degree, stay in the community or the region. Therefore, it becomes critical for the college to create that positive learning environment the first time for students to build that lifelong learning relationship.

Relationships are important for community education and workforce development. Individuals who enroll in, say, art classes and find the experience amazing will gain an appreciation of the college. That same individual who enjoys the relationship by taking community education classes may contribute to the college foundation. It is all circular because each relationship reinforces others.

According to Rio Salado College President Chris Bustamante of Tempe, Arizona:

> In Arizona, Rio Salado College is part of the Maricopa County Community College District, which is the largest provider of workforce training in the state. Part of the district's mission is for its colleges to be engaged in workforce development within our local and regional communities, and we are making a significant impact.
>
> I can give you examples of the roles that the community colleges play in workforce development. First, I'll share information about a systems perspective and then how workforce development drives aspects of our work. There are 10 independent, accredited colleges as part of the Maricopa system that serves about 250,000 students each year. At this level, we have a workforce development office led by an Associate Vice Chancellor who is supported by a team. They research job and career data and other issues which guide relevant career programming curriculum and degree and certificate programs.
>
> This team also works with the Greater Phoenix Economic Council, which recruits companies to the Phoenix metropolitan area. We are a large training arm of that economic council whose members come from different municipalities and government entities from all over the 9,200-square-mile county.
>
> The workforce development office then brings forward the needs that employers have and refers companies to the various colleges that specialize in that training. There is a connection between what the needs are and which community college in the system is best suited to meet that demand. The district also created a corporate college a year and a half ago, similar to what Tony Zeiss has done as the President of Central Piedmont Community College, located in the Charlotte, North Carolina, regional area.
>
> At the time, President Zeiss came to consult and speak to us on how to establish a college dedicated to workforce training. Under this model, businesses can call upon the corporate college and say, "I have a particular need. Can you broker ways to meet my need within the college system?" We now have a corporate college that primarily does noncredit work but, if needed, will connect employers and students to the various credit-based programs within the Maricopa Community Colleges.
>
> We also have articulation agreements at the district level with many private and public colleges and universities. Everyone benefits from these agreements and that's a good thing. The system helps us coordinate everyone within it. All of the community colleges in the system, residents, and students can take advantage of these agreements that provide seamless pathways to other higher education institutions.
>
> Rio Salado College serves 30 business and industry partners as an independent institution within the Maricopa District. We have a dedicated partnership team that works with our workforce partners to develop customized programs, certificate programs, and degree pathways for companies that qualify. Companies that we serve include US Airways (now American Airlines), USAA, and organizations with call-center operations.
>
> We partner with companies that provide in-house training such as flight training, ramp operations, or law enforcement training. As an example, police

cadets can earn up to 39 credits, which lead to a certificate of completion from Rio Salado when they graduate from their respective academies. They can then apply these credits or certificate toward an associate in applied science degree in law enforcement technology. Upon completion of a two-year degree, employees often become eligible for career advancements with their employer.

Our relationship with Cox Communications demonstrates the level of impact that our partnerships have. Rio Salado has partnered with Cox since 2001 to provide customized training for their employees. To date we have served about 5,800 students, and awarded over 46,000 credits. We have also awarded over 2,600 certificates and generated about $3.1 million in tuition revenue.

Palatine, Illinois–based William Rainey Harper College President Ken Ender emphasizes the importance of community colleges as part of a network. He points out:

Part of the work of the community college is to identify with the network of other community assets so that, by fusing those assets together, you get the capacity to build a system of workforce development. The community college might be the broker of the system and one member of the system. But I think it's hard to imagine that economic development, education, and workforce development are not intertwined.

Community colleges bring the parties together that represent those assets, sometimes leading or being part of those conversations. We've done work in manufacturing over the last four years and have built a credentialing ladder that allows students to learn and earn simultaneously. The students move through steps and certificates that ultimately bridge to an associate degree in manufacturing, and that bridges to a baccalaureate degree.

The program was developed by employers or industry, if you will, and by school superintendents because we have a connection to secondary schools for early college credit. As part of economic development, we try to locate this program around the state strategically in 23 communities to support manufacturers' interests statewide. It is a comprehensive program that no one institution can do alone. Ultimately, it's a footprint that integrates schools and communities with economic and workforce leaders.

Kenosha, Wisconsin–based Gateway Technical College Vice President of Business and Workforce Solutions Deborah Davidson sees community colleges cast in many roles:

I think community colleges play many roles. I meet with companies and find out what their needs are. I also meet with organizations that represent employers. Gateway is located in the Milwaukee 7 service area, which includes Milwaukee and the six counties surrounding it. Many regional groups are working on talent acquisition and talent development across several industries, which can provide more of a macro—or industry—view of the region's needs. When we meet one-on-one with employers and listen to their specific needs we can then determine if they fit into the macro and there is a previously developed solution we can provide or if the needs are specialized and require a more customized training solution.

We also join our economic development partners during various stages of their business recruitment activities. We attend these meetings because one of the first questions employers ask is "What does the talent pool look like?" If the talent isn't at the level the employer needs it to be, they want to know what systems are in place to get them to that level. The two-year college is a great resource for these employers both for academic programs and customized short-term training for their incumbent workforce or preparing new hires.

We collaborate with our job center/career one-stops. For example, when they hold job fairs for employers, we have a booth and provide information for those who may not meet the requirements of the positions being hired for. Our programs and services oftentimes can assist that job seeker in upskilling and/or preparing to get a job at the next job fair.

Lakewood, Washington–based Clover Park Technical College Special Assistant to the President Mabel Edmonds also supports the idea of the community college as part of a network: "Community and technical colleges are key partners in the workforce development system by providing education, training, and other services. They can serve as conveners, facilitators, and hubs for the activities needed to implement effective and efficient systems."

Cleveland, Ohio–based Cuyahoga Community College Executive Vice President of Workforce, Community, and Economic Development William Gary adds to the perspective offered by Edmonds:

> I believe community colleges should be the "prime providers" of workforce development training and education and serve as conveners and facilitators for all business and community stakeholders involved in developing workforce policy, strategy, metrics, and outcomes. Community college workforce curriculum, training, programs, and services should be aligned with the in-demand needs of businesses, thus leading to jobs that pay livable and sustainable wages.
>
> Community colleges should focus, primarily, on addressing the needs of those industry sectors that drive the economy, and ensure "pipelines" of qualified individuals to meet these needs via partnerships with K–12s and community based organizations. Key to these partnerships is early communication of in-demand occupations and the knowledge, skills, abilities, and soft skills required to become prepared and successful in the workplace. So the community college, given its mission and its vision, ought to be at the forefront of the workforce development agenda.
>
> Let me give you an example. During the past 20 months, since I arrived at Cuyahoga Community College, I have recognized that Cleveland, and Northeast Ohio in general, is experiencing an economic resurgence that extends beyond its historical manufacturing footprint. Part of that has to be attributed to the growth in the hospitality industry. To make sure that our community college was aligned with this sector growth, I invited members of the hospital-

ity industry, primarily hotel general managers, to meet with me to discuss their workforce challenges and issues. All accepted, and for about three hours, including lunch, we talked about their challenges and issues as individuals, organizations, and as an industry.

My purpose was to assess how we could assist them in addressing both short- and long-term priorities through customized training and credentialing, currently being offered through our Hospitality Management Program, and provide jobs to the hundreds of unemployed and underserved seeking a better life. After considerable discussion, the general managers all agreed to participate in a Cuyahoga Community College–led industry sector approach to recruiting and training candidates for employment.

The hoteliers indicated this was the first time in history that anyone from a community college had invited them to share their views and offer assistance to meet their workforce and profit-and-loss goals. As a result, we have developed a five-week Boot Camp training program to prepare and to train individuals for the hospitality industry, both front-line and office jobs and in anticipation of the Republican National Convention that will be convening in Cleveland in three months.

We also wanted to sustain their industry growth beyond the Republican National Convention. That's the role I believe community colleges ought to play. But we've got to produce. So now we have engaged community-based organizations to help identify potential employees to be trained. We have completed training of the first cohort of individuals who received certificates of completion and are currently being interviewed and hired by employers. We're going to do three more cohorts between now and the Republican National Convention. And we are doing the same thing for public safety police and fire organizations.

We took the initiative and went to them to express that we have a vested interest in the economic well-being of Cleveland and Northeast Ohio. And we want to contribute (we are not here to sell you anything but are here to listen; I am here to identify your needs) and if I can put together a solution for you, would you be willing to engage the community college? And that's what we are doing!

It's important to me that the business community understand that the community college can't do everything alone. We are trainers and educators but not social agencies. So we do not only have to understand the demand side but understand and anticipate the supply side. It is important to communicate what the demands are, showing that the community college has a solution for individuals seeking not only training and education but support and "wraparound" services to ensure success throughout that process. We are going to accomplish this with the Urban League, with the NAACP, philanthropic, workforce investment boards, and other community youth-based organizations, all of which will have a role to play. Each is accountable to make sure that the respective roles are carried out. That's how we are doing it!

I believe we are well positioned, from a workforce development standpoint, to understand the business community, to understand the plight of students coming to our doors, and to understand that a growing economy requires all its citizens to participate. It is not possible to sustain growth with half of the population.

Here in Cleveland, we have a significantly impoverished community that needs to be included, outreached, explained to, and communicated with about opportunities to help them successfully move into the economic mainstream. That's the mission the community college has adopted throughout the country. Certainly, some of us do a better job than others. But Cuyahoga Community College is so entrenched in the community, and we are so fortunate to have a president of our institution that "gets it," the importance of workforce development as integral to the college's mission. I didn't leave Virginia to come here to sleep! I transitioned here to make a difference and add value to the great work that preceded me.

Chapter Four

The Community College Role in Community Development, Economic Development, Individual Career Counseling, and Training

We asked the community college Thought Leaders for their perspectives on the role that community colleges should play in community development, economic development, individual career counseling, and training. We did that because we believe that training only works if placed in the right context. Although the Thought Leaders had something to say about these issues in the previous chapter, they embellished on their thoughts when asked specifically about these other issues.

"There are many roles community colleges can play," began Kenosha, Wisconsin–based Gateway Technical College President and Chief Executive Bryan Albrecht. He went on:

> One is workforce development. But our role is bigger than that. In economic development, we look at our community colleges as bringing new resources to the community, and state and federal grants allow us to leverage training capacity and adapt to changing talent needs. Product development is one area where we work closely with our local and regional businesses to leverage the capacity.
>
> Another strategy is business incubation and entrepreneurship: I think it's critical, and many community colleges are involved in developing opportunities for new businesses to flourish. We host a business incubator site, and we have faculty, students, and intellectual property readily available. We've developed what's called an accelerator program for small business start-ups. If a large company has a new product it wants to launch, we partner with them. If

it's a small business trying to get off the ground, we develop funding mecha-
nisms and align venture capitalists. And if it's a training issue, we try to align
new services and bring in new, additional funds to support the training.

Brooklyn Park, Minnesota–based Hennepin Technical College President
Merrell Irving emphasized the importance of serving students. As he explained:

> Every path helps students improve themselves. By that I mean not for the
> student to just engage in a community or technical college but to persist and
> complete. Success could be that students enroll and later decide they want to
> attend a university; the students enroll and earn an industry-recognized certifi-
> cate; or they enroll, and they earn the skills and qualifications leading to
> employment.
>
> The community or technical college's role is to provide all that. It serves
> everyone in the community and exists to educate people within the commu-
> nity. Community and technical colleges play a crucial role in a local commu-
> nity's economic development by bringing local people together around the
> common topic of business development and helping them learn successful
> practices from each other.
>
> Economic development stems from workforce development. A company
> cannot grow unless it possesses the workforce to meet its existing and future
> needs. The same is true to attract new employers to the local area, region, or
> state. These issues are interconnected. It is in connecting the points of most
> concern. It is community development; it is economic development; and it is
> also customized community business counseling.
>
> Community and technical colleges are the local economic generators for
> municipalities and the state. Most individuals that come to community or
> technical colleges commute, and they will be the ones that are most likely to
> continue on to a university. They will be the most likely to remain employed in
> the local municipality, area, and state. Community and technical colleges real-
> ly must be taken 10 times more seriously for the impact they have on the local
> and regional areas.
>
> Community and technical colleges provide for employer–employee reten-
> tion through skills development and the opportunity for lifelong learning pro-
> grams. Community and technical colleges have the most direct relationships
> with employers. While universities pride themselves on research, community
> colleges provide for the direct application of learning and skills development.
> Employers act in tandem with the community or technical college to identify,
> and meet, local workforce development needs. Key issues are who we compete
> with and what we must do to continue to meet local needs.
>
> Community and technical colleges can answer that question of *how*. How
> soon, and who's involved, what do we need to compete successfully? Commu-
> nity and technical colleges can perform in a course-per-credit or noncredit
> perspective. The bottom line is that community and technical colleges can
> answer that need for successful local and regional impact. One significant
> difference between a community or technical college and university is that a

community or technical college is not an exclusive institution and tries to accommodate varying degrees of academic readiness.

Community and technical colleges admit everyone from the traditional-age student to the nontraditional-age student, the adult learner to the single parent, the veteran, English-as-a-second-language learner, those needing literacy skills, or the disabled, and offer various programs for those completing the GED, transfer students, and other opportunities that create pathways for the local community. Community and technical colleges try to meet the needs of all local citizens. They make it happen for any student who wants to gain the knowledge and skills needed to join the workforce.

Community and technical colleges raise the economic and educational levels of the local area and help attract industry. When you look at enrollments of community or technical colleges, you find they serve many roles. They help people transition into the workforce, facilitate movement within the workplace, and provide advancement opportunities for those within the workplace. Community and technical colleges play an important intermediary role with all players at the table—that is, chambers of commerce, CEOs representing community-based organizations, local leaders, and others. Community and technical colleges are positioned at the center of the table.

Community and technical colleges should pride themselves on being great neighbors and responsible corporate citizens. They contribute to the well-being of their communities through charitable giving, employee volunteerism, and civic leadership. Their dedication as a community partner is also evidenced in the local events they sponsor. These roles are apparent in the conversations held between designated local community liaisons and area residents.

In the struggle to maintain a vibrant economy and develop good jobs, communities are increasingly turning to a local resource for innovative, flexible, and timely assistance: the community or technical college. Over the past 10 years, there has been a significant increase in the involvement of community and technical colleges in economic development. It appears to be a trend with growing momentum.

Since the mid-1980s community and technical colleges across the nation have stepped forward to meet the challenge of helping their communities grow jobs and develop the workforce. While most community colleges began with a mission to serve the community with low-cost, accessible educational programs, they have often found that their mission was tied not only to the educational goals of their students but also to the health of the community's economy.

Many technical colleges, founded to help meet the explosion of new technology in the workplace, saw this connection earlier than some broadly structured community colleges. But the message over the past decade has been clear in enrollments and educational goals: community and technical colleges are providing adults the academic, workforce, and career development skills they need. Meeting the needs of the students is only part of the equation, however.

Community and technical colleges are also meeting the needs of business, industry, and economic development, helping to create better-paying jobs for the members of their communities. And a subset of the colleges, those with advanced technology centers as part of their programs, seems to do the best job of marrying service to students with service to business, industry, and economic development. All of that makes for a platform for community and economic development.

Charlotte, North Carolina–based Central Piedmont Community College President P. Anthony Zeiss sees the issues of community development, economic development, individual career counseling, and training as being related to globalization. As he explains:

Basically, the question is, how are you going to become global? We have determined that we will build on the impact we have had. We are ranked #2 in finance in the nation; we are #1 in energy in the nation, and we were recently named the sixth-busiest airport in the world. We also have fine health care and educational facilities; but we remain vulnerable to economic downturns.

During the last recession, we lost 30,000 finance jobs overnight. We want to broaden our economic base and become more global. In doing that we can better identify that we have to become more proficient in advanced manufacturing; better at recruiting and training folks in intermodal transportation or the movement of goods; and better at helping entrepreneurs with starting new businesses, because most new jobs begin with entrepreneurs (you know, like Steve Jobs).

How can we become the global hub of commerce? By being the best in the country for *creating* things? That's innovation and small business development. At *making* things? That's manufacturing. At *moving* things? That's transportation. We've put together a strategic plan, and we are implementing it now.

The Panama Canal has got us moving because we want to make sure that we can take advantage of the huge Post-Panamax ships that come in here. We have a dual-lane highway and no stoplights between here (Charlotte, North Carolina) and Savannah, Georgia, and from here to Charleston, South Carolina. The cities have been investing much money (a half billion to one billion dollars) into those ports—and that's vital for economic development. There are also smaller ports at Wilmington, North Carolina; Beaufort, South Carolina; and Norfolk, Virginia. It is the East Coast compared to California. Very few ships will stop in California and ship by truck or rail to the East Coast; rather, they will come here, and we want to make sure that we are ready for it.

Increasingly, inbound cargo is transferred directly from an ocean vessel to railcars and then transported to an inland location, away from the most congested port itself, for further processing and distribution. These inland areas, or intermodal centers, serve as "inland ports," with some handling as much cargo volume as their coastal counterparts. Charlotte is already on the relatively short list of current areas widely recognized as full-fledged inland ports. Though the inland port concept is not new, these locations are becoming increasingly critical to the global supply chain, affecting logistics decisions ranging from shipping routes to warehouse locations.

We believe that we have to be involved in the supply business because we are providing a world-class workforce for employers. But it's deeper than that. We also need to be participating in the demand side of the equation by helping to recruit jobs for people. We can assist the economic developers to recruit jobs, and we in the community college world have been doing that for years. We are center stage to prove to employers we can provide them a skilled workforce.

We find that community colleges must help our cities and regions develop an economic vision and assemble the proper leaders to develop competitive assets to achieve that vision.

I have two important litmus-test questions I always ask at the end of every discussion on new curriculum, new programs, new procedures, or new policies. The first question is this: *Is this good for our students?* The second question is this: *Is this good for our community?* They are tied together! I mean you can't have one without the other; they are inextricably linked. Human development is economic development.

If we are preparing a world-class workforce, we have to influence both labor supply and demand. How do you put together a world-class workforce? We must have the workforce in our vision. Our vision at Central Piedmont Community College is to "become the nation's leader in workforce development." That vision is very clear to business leaders, policy makers, deans, faculty, the board, and the entire community. We are about the business of preparing people for jobs. Some jobs are in theater and the arts; some are in technology; some are in services. But it's all workforce development because it's all human development.

Sumiton, Alabama–based Bevill State Community College President Larry A. Ferguson sees the community college role as being centered in the community. As he explains:

We are highly committed to community development. Because community development also has a very strong link to economic development, you must have the quality of life and place within your community for the economy to thrive. Some of what we do around community development is based on cultural appreciation—everything from the theater to music.

In many of our communities, the role of the community college is to be the hub of that activity. We are also heavily involved in kids' camps, and I say that from a perspective of science, technology, engineering, and math [STEM]. We have a program called Career Craze where we try to encourage students to enter those areas of the industry sectors we serve at an early age—in middle school—and sometimes even before that. I think all of that is community development.

Early-college models or dual-credit models are also part of community development in which we and other community colleges are heavily involved. We try to inspire students in secondary schools into getting additional credentials and certifications to ensure that they succeed. That program can be a game changer in the local economy. Community development is a component, or a facet, of economic development.

Now economic development, as we talked already a little bit about, stems from workforce development. Companies cannot expand or grow unless they have the workforce to fit their needs. The same is true to entice different companies into your state. They are all linked. You know, it is like connecting the dots. It is community development, it is economic development, and it is also—as you mentioned—their individualized career counseling; that is honestly something we want to do better, so it is part of our new strategic plan for 2016 to 2022. Our system will focus on job placement, on that career job link, because many of our students do not understand what it is like to go into manufacturing today.

As an example, working in manufacturing was always a dark and dirty career for our grandfathers. That is not the case now. It is highly technical and specialized. It is a clean environment with excellent jobs and high wages. We need to do a better job of informing our students about multiple options beyond those that are obvious, like health care. We need to support health care as one of the largest industry segments. But there is work beyond that—like manufacturing. We want to make sure that young people understand coming out of secondary schools there are multiple options for them to participate in and have a very successful career.

When I was in Kentucky, our community colleges partnered with the Kentucky Association of Manufacturing. Toyota and Bluegrass Community and Technical College came together to form a unique model as part of our industrial maintenance technician program. They called it Advanced Manufacturing Technician, but it employs students in an earn-and-learn component, so that students go to class two days a week and then work three days a week in sponsoring companies that pay them an average wage of $26,000 per year while they are in college. They can walk away and not have any student debt. I think that is the example. And that has grown.

It succeeded in central Kentucky. We now have six chapters of Kentucky FAME—the Kentucky Federation for Advanced Manufacturing Education. When these companies come together, they form a real partnership between the companies, the KCTCS institutions, and the students. There is power in an earn-and-learn model—which is really an apprenticeship or internship model. We have known that for years. The best idea is to link employers with students to provide them with support and move them up a career pathway. The outcomes have been significant. I think that is a good example of a partnership between the private sector and community colleges. It ensures community colleges meet community, economic development, and individual career needs.

I think we have to get better. Workforce development is centered on relationships. We should have brutally honest, open relationships with business and industry clients. We need to know if what we deliver in our classrooms, through customized training or traditional academic-credit curricula, truly builds the competencies those students and employers need to succeed in a particular industry sector. We can always improve relationship management.

I will share another example. We are so committed to relationship management that, as a system and for close to two years, we have been using a customer relationship management [CRM] tool called Salesforce.com that is well known outside of higher education. Just like they do in the private sector, we use a customer relationship management tool to track those relationships to make sure we get the right feedback. We also use tools such as DACUM

[Developing a Curriculum], Delphi studies, and others to align the competencies we seek within our curriculum.

Different industry sectors want not just a credential from us but want students to achieve an industry credential. We partner with them to make sure that we align our programs to industry credentialing requirements.

Blytheville-based Arkansas Northeastern College President James Shemwell adds support to the views of others already mentioned but emphasizes the individual's importance. As he observes:

Regarding community development, I see our role as one of building economic competence to help people reach their desired quality of life. What I mean by that is not so much teaching them economics—and I will confess that I am an old economics teacher—but let's help people build a skill set that can help them compete in the marketplace. Let's help them to work and get a job so they have choices in life. That's what I tell people repeatedly. Money is not everything, but money gives students choices. Like it or not, money gives students freedom. The less money students have, the less freedom they have. It is just a fact of life.

Regarding economic development, what I would say is that if local employers do not tell the college story, the college is doing something wrong. If companies or businesses come into your community, and if representatives of companies won't tell the college story for you, then the college is doing something wrong.

If that is not happening, that is charge number one regarding what we ought to do. We ought to make sure that our employers are singing our song or telling our story. The way we do that is we talk to them, listen to them, and solve the problems they face. They ought to be our biggest champions. We are fortunate here, locally, that that is the case.

We ought to do career counseling on the first day that students walk in the door. I formerly was Dean for Technical Programs here and the students, as part of their graduation process, would have to come by and see me. I would sign their graduation forms and verify that they had met the requirements and all of that. I can't tell you how often I would see just an ashen look on students' faces when I would ask them, "What are you going to do now? What does the future look like for you; what kind of job do you think you will get?" And they just had this look wash over them, and they would say, in a hundred ways, "I wish I knew at the beginning what I know now. I wouldn't have pursued this. I didn't know what the work environment was going to be like."

That information is available. It is available up front. Since I became president, we changed admission standards. We also make sure that every student seeking a certificate or degree meets with one of three advisors their first semester and maybe during their first year if they are developmental. But they meet with one of three advisors. We are a small institution. Last year we averaged about 1,400 students per semester, 1,400 to 1,500. We are down. We used to be about 2,000, but the economy has gotten better, so our numbers are down. But that is how we can get by with three people.

There is the Transfer Advisor; there is a Career and Technical Education Advisor; and there is an Allied Health Advisor. Depending on the students' initial area of interest, they will see one of those three people. They must fill out a short little form that asks questions about what they are interested in. It asks what does this pay and what the job growth prospects are for this. How a student could answer that is because they have someone there to facilitate and direct them to informative websites. The Department of Labor website is one place that contains this information.

Let's see what this pays, number one. Let's make sure this is the quality of life we are envisioning for ourselves. Does this match our expectations? Let's make sure that is the case. Let them read about what the work environment is like and what they will have to do. Let them see what the education requirements are. Does the job require a bachelor's degree, or does it require something less than that? Finally, what are the growth prospects? Is it a growing field, or is it one where the student will compete with many people for what few jobs are available? These are the questions to be discussing with students on the first day they are in college.

If there is one thing that colleges must do a much better job of, it is this. We need to start people on the right track with something that is in demand and has a future. When I talk to high school students, I'll ask a question. Sometimes I play a game with them. We have many little gimmick pins here we give away as promotional items. Some look like airplanes for the aviation maintenance program. We have one that looks like a hypodermic syringe for the allied health programs.

I tell them if they answer this question, I will give them one of these pins. Then I'll ask, "How much money do you think a registered nurse makes?" You will hear the responses—and they are not that much. How much do you think a welder makes? Well, it is this. How much do you think someone with a bachelor's degree in history makes? They will answer $100,000 or $150,000. I tell them to drop to what is realistic and they are shocked to learn that nurses and welders make more money.

We are doing students such a disservice by not at least informing them of their choices. Let them make an informed choice. If they will go into a field that does not have legitimate job prospects, that pays little money, let them know that up front. It is a deeper issue. It is not one of your questions, but we really ought to think about how we invest our limited resources. We ought to advise students to move into in-demand fields.

Prestonsburg, Kentucky–based Big Sandy Community and Technical College President Devin Stephenson emphasizes the role of community colleges in community development:

Community development is fundamental to our mission. Without community development there can be no economic development—it is the prerequisite. As an institution we should find ourselves in the very fiber and the fabric of the communities we serve. We should work to make a difference in improving the infrastructure, in improving education, in improving the social life of our communities, and in exercising our civic responsibility as a good corporate citizen.

As a community leader, it is up to me to develop our leadership team into a unit that understands engagement and the importance of external involvement and influence. I believe that is where many institutions of higher education in the past have failed. They have withdrawn from an external focus and have not effectively engaged in their service area's ecosystem. Doing that is critical. I think we have to be engaged; we have to influence and develop relationships and make meaningful connections throughout the regions we serve.

As far as economic development, communities are increasingly turning to us for innovative, flexible, and timely assistance. What we are seeing is that businesses and industries are reaching out for assistance. I can tell you, over the past 15 years, there has been a significant increase in the involvement of community and technical colleges in community and economic development, and it is going to become even more important. Why? Because as a higher education sector we have the ability and mind-set to adapt to an ever-changing world and global economy. However, we must be focused on the needs of business and industry—both now and in the future.

Since the mid-1980s, community and technical colleges across the nation have stepped forward to meet the challenges of assisting communities to grow jobs and develop their workforce. The community colleges began with a mission to serve the community with low-cost, accessible programs. They often found that their mission was tied not only to the academic and educational goals of the students but also to the health of the community's economy.

Many technical colleges were founded to help the explosion of new technology. They saw this connection earlier than did other sectors of higher education; I know we did at our technical college in Alabama. We saw the trend coming before Alabama even had comprehensive community colleges. But the message over the past 15 years has been clear, and it has been clear in our enrollments and our changing educational priorities—and it is that community and technical colleges are providing adults with the academic, workforce, and career development skills they need and that are demanded by today's business and industry.

Let me say, too, that meeting the needs of students is one part of the equation. Community and technical colleges also are meeting the needs of business, industry, and economic development leaders and recruiters, and government. Our focus is creating job opportunities for this region. Underemployed individuals come to us because they want a better quality of life, and they know if they get a course, certification, and/or degree, they can advance.

Individual career counseling, success coaching, and navigation are critical. It is more important now than ever before because of the need to streamline the career pathway. Career counseling should embody two basic components: intrusive advising and student success coaching or navigation. Student success coaching that focuses holistically on a student's life and student development—the whole piece—is critically important. We are seeing more students who are attempting to manage multiple priorities and greater demands on their lives and they simply need someone to listen and provide meaningful coaching to get through tough personal times or a hurdle they are facing in a course or program.

For training, I believe it is vital not only for students entering the work-force but to those incumbent workers who simply want to upgrade their skills. I think that is where we do our best work. Community colleges really become all things to all people. As open-access, open-door-admissions institutions, we take people from all walks of life, and then we diligently work to create success stories out of each and every one of them. That's what I like to call "making a difference," and nothing is more fulfilling than to see a candidate walk across the stage at commencement having achieved their educational goal.

Unfortunately, I don't think some community college presidents view their role with the same external perspective. They become engrossed in the internal "role" and fail to realize that relevancy and possibilities occur when external engagement is a priority.

According to Moorefield-based Eastern West Virginia Community and Technical College President Charles Terrell, involvement is the key to suc-cess. As he explains:

My biggest piece of advice, and I know for college presidents we struggle with balancing internal and external stakeholders, my advice would be to get in-volved with external stakeholders as much as possible. Those external rela-tionships link to community development.

On a more personal note, I am the President of the Hardy County Chamber of Commerce. That gives me the opportunity to interact with the community and understand what are the opportunities and the challenges that the commu-nities are facing. We have to ask, How can the college be involved in commu-nity development as a partner? As we look at shrinking state appropriations, partnerships are becoming such an important piece of what community col-leges should do.

Being engaged with the community—and that leads to another part—how can community leaders be supportive? Community leaders know of commu-nity development at the college, and if the college leadership is involved, they will speak highly of it to other stakeholders. In my role as President of the Chamber, we had a conversation with the West Virginia Development Office this week about On-Track, which is a first-level program of the Main Street program. That's a national program. Its focus is on what would be one or two strategic, important community development projects. Two communities in our county are interested in the On-Track program. During the conversation, one Chamber member said, "You know that we have a community college locally."

We had two communities, and I proposed to the Chamber that the college could host the seminar on the On-Track application for both communities. That way the college could partner with both communities. The relationship is important.

For economic development, in 2012, the college hosted an economic de-velopment summit. We serve six counties, and we invited our economic devel-opment directors from those six counties. Included in the summit were super-intendents from the public school systems, career and technical education directors, the staff of workforce development and other departments of the college. For us in education, we met quarterly, but we had never engaged economic development directors. At the summit, we asked what is happening in your county, what keeps you up at night about economic development, where do you see your opportunities, where do you see challenges, and do you see any partnerships helping you with opportunities and addressing those challenges.

The outcome was that the economic development directors said they wanted to meet with educational representatives from that point on because it was a valuable discussion. From that, we developed priorities. Six counties identified small business development. They also recognized the need to market the region and not just one county. The college is now seen as facilitating this regional discussion on economic development. We are now operating a small business incubator to promote small business development in the region as a direct consequence of that summit. We also have a full-time Entrepreneur in Residence.

The college should be a facilitator for economic development because economic development directors acknowledge that they cannot sustain business and industry, nor will they be able to recruit new business and industry, without the skilled workforce. The college, secondary school systems, and the career technical centers within our region are critical in meeting that workforce need.

According to Tempe, Arizona–based Rio Salado College President Chris Bustamante:

> The community college has an important role in community and economic development. We have a dental hygiene school and dental assistant program. We partner with the dental community and the local dental foundation through these programs, which support students with internships and practicum opportunities.
>
> We also have teacher education programs that partner with school districts to make sure that preservice teachers have practicum experiences as well. Each year we host a job fair for teachers and invite schools from all over the state to come to our conference center. Students come prepared with résumés to be interviewed on the spot. In many cases they are offered a teaching contract at the event.
>
> Another example is the insurance industry. Recently the Arizona Insurance Council asked us to develop a certificate and degree program for their sector. We began the process by developing elements that are common for the whole industry—meeting the foundational knowledge and basic courses students need as part of a certificate program and industry-related exams. Industry leaders such as State Farm, Progressive Insurance, and others are thrilled and plan to provide scholarships for the program. They receive value from sharing their expertise to develop the curriculum, and partnering with us to offer students opportunities for internships. Students who complete the program can become qualified candidates for hire or career advancement.

Palatine, Illinois–based William Rainey Harper College President Ken Ender emphasizes how the community college is regarded in its community context. As he notes:

> Often we [community colleges] are viewed as a community asset without an agenda. We are a neutral voice. We have convening capacity. I think that's one role that presidents can take up uniquely. I think "convening and champion-ing" are the two Cs that I'd include in this role. It is a unique role in many communities to have an institution positioned to reach across, down, and up to bring together all interested stakeholders in the community, economic, and workforce development process.
>
> Let me provide an example. Our Learn and Earn program was unique. It was not always there. We developed it with all the characteristics to attract the stakeholders to the table. My instinct about leadership is that, if we bring the interested parties to the table and provide them with all the same information so that all are working from the same scorecard, we will get much better solutions than any one group could accomplish alone.
>
> Using our convening role, we organized a daylong summit on manufactur-ing and assembled leaders of businesses, secondary and postsecondary schools, and economic development in our region. We spent a day examining the issues affecting the supply-side-of-labor challenge for these manufacturers. We came out of that event with a clear vision we needed to establish proactive ways to drive the talent pipeline. It took about a year to put together a solu-tion—about 12 or 13 of us developing a curriculum based on the competencies developed by the National Manufacturing Association. Eventually, we devised a clear pathway through certifications that resulted in a degree. We then used that to apply for a grant to diffuse the curriculum statewide to a network of other community colleges to encourage them to go through similar activities in their communities. It worked out well.

American Association of Community Colleges Senior Vice President Jen Worth explains that

> there is no wrong door to a community college. Every door helps students improve themselves. We count success in many ways. Success could be that the student enrolls but later attends a four-year institution. Success could mean that the student enrolls and earns an industry-recognized certificate to work at a specific job. Success could also mean students enroll and then find employ-ment.
>
> The community college's role is to do all that and more. The institutions try to serve everyone in the community because a local community college is there to educate people in that community. Our students are not as transient or mobile, and they tend to stay in their communities and improve the tax base of the community. Whether a student goes on to a four-year college, gets a job, or simply becomes more educated, the community college is performing commu-nity and economic development because it is improving the workforce devel-opment level by improving the educational level of that local and regional area. They're performing economic development because they are creating a

more talented workforce in that region that will eventually increase their tax base.

Community colleges help individuals succeed by offering many support services. If the community college does not offer those services in their own facilities, they have access to services through their networks of workforce investment boards, community and faith-based organizations, and collaborative entities. Community colleges across the country are offering various diversified services, though they may look differently in Samoa than in Houston. AACC's members exist in settings that range from rural to urban. They may look and feel very different in different places, but the underpinnings are always the same. We engage students because we are flexible and adaptable; we provide more offerings and all the right support for students and employers.

Kenosha, Wisconsin–based Gateway Technical College Vice President of Business and Workforce Solutions Deborah Davidson addressed the community college's role in community, economic, and career development and training by offering an example of how the issues are intertwined:

An example of community development in the Gateway District is located in the city of Racine, a city with the highest unemployment rate in our state. It is a co-working space called Launch Box, and it is designed for individuals who have outgrown the table at Starbucks where they are working on their laptops.

People are looking for a space to work outside their homes, but they want an atmosphere where they can meet customers and engage with other entrepreneurs or business start-ups. In a co-working space people become members, similar to a gym membership. The space includes desks and work spaces, Wi-Fi, two conference rooms, and other amenities that meet the members' needs. We currently have over 125 members who use the co-working space, or attend on-site networking or lunch-and-learn events where they can access advice and input from experts in marketing, accounting, or other related small business topics.

Different than a business incubator, not all Launch Box members will graduate and move on to a brick-and-mortar location. Some will grow and create jobs, others will remain sole proprietorships that need a location where they can meet their customers. Launch Box members interact with our business students who can assist with a special project or launch their own business.

We are helping people understand there are opportunities for them to own their own businesses. Gateway's Launch Box received U.S. SBA [Small Business Administration] funding to offer a "Growth Accelerator" where eight business start-ups participated in a 12-week program that included mentoring, and a curriculum to further develop their business plan to take their product or service to commercialization. Successful completers received a $10,000 grant for their business start-up. We plan to offer a second Growth Accelerator with a focus on women, veterans, and underserved populations. Economic development and workforce development are integrated and complementary as we are developing individuals; they *are* the workforce and they contribute to the economy.

Lakewood, Washington–based Clover Park Technical College Special Assistant to the President Mabel Edmonds summarized: "The college should, and does, participate actively in our workforce development council, partner with all key stakeholders in the workforce system, take part in economic development planning activities, and host activities for the community. We provide career counseling, education/training, and focus on the underserved and underrepresented in our community, including people of color, the homeless, and others."

Chapter Five

Present and Future Barriers and Challenges Faced by Community Colleges in Carrying Out Their Roles

Few observers of contemporary education in the U.S. would dispute that educational institutions at all levels face many barriers and challenges. That is as true of community colleges as it is of other educational institutions. We asked the Thought Leaders about what they perceive to be the barriers and challenges community colleges face in carrying out their roles.

Kenosha, Wisconsin–based Gateway Technical College President and Chief Executive Bryan Albrecht sees "regionalism as one challenge. We serve, and are limited to, three counties. Yet we have programs that have earned national recognition, and we could recruit nationally. But we must stay within our local geographical region. Regionalism can be a positive and a negative force. We have to become more entrepreneurial because of changes in the economy and changes in governmental funding to support education (at all levels) and community colleges (specifically). But when we face limits on our regional reach, it's hard to be more entrepreneurial. There are challenges that way, trying to balance the entrepreneurial side with a publicly funded model that has been put in place with community colleges."

In a refrain repeated by many Thought Leaders, Brooklyn Park, Minnesota–based Hennepin Technical College President Merrell Irving noted that "one big challenge, honestly, as you have probably heard, is funding. Although we are asked to do more things in our community and technical colleges, our funding is being cut. It is much harder to deliver the training and services the community needs without the necessary funding to do it."

Sumiton, Alabama–based Bevill State Community College President Larry A. Ferguson emphasized the same point:

> Funding is a big challenge. Community colleges are facing funding cuts even as they are asked to do more. It is much harder to deliver the training and services we need to offer without that funding support. Kentucky is fortunate because the legislature has been committed to allocating dollars to offset the cost of some training for our companies, and that is very helpful. But will that continue?
>
> Private-sector companies often cut training. It can be a vicious circle. They cut the training and then don't have the qualified workforce they need, and the bottom line is affected. One big challenge is to maintain adequate funding for community technical colleges across the United States to ensure that they can deliver those services.
>
> I think we should applaud President Obama. We have had so much attention during this president's administration because his administration has realized the direct connection between building skills and community technical colleges. We hope that commitment will continue as national and state administrations change. Funding is the biggest challenge that our colleges face.

Warren, Michigan–based Macomb Community College President James Jacobs noted that

> there are many barriers. They are the usual suspects of money, resources, time, and effort. Those are important, but three significant barriers are worth describing. The first one is the tendency to see workforce development as separate from the institution. If we go to any community college in the country, they always say they do workforce development, and they have a Dean or Vice President of Workforce Development and a Dean of Technology. Usually, these functions are on one side of the institution and liberal arts is on the other side. Then, within the workforce development function, a distinction is usually made between credit and noncredit classes and programs. I detest the term "noncredit" because it sounds derogatory, like the idea or program is worthless.
>
> If all learning is learning, all aspects of a college should have a workforce component. That is one principle of student success—employment and earnings. That is why people go to school. All community college student success efforts should include some form of employment opportunity at the end. That barrier—the tendency to see students' success as something which means going on to a four-year school or just getting your degree—must be modified to include employment and earnings as part of student success. That is the first.
>
> A second barrier centers on staffing and skill sets. We hire people both in the faculty ranks and the administrative ranks who increasingly have academic credentials but may not come out of the industry or the sector we are most involved in. Community colleges must pride themselves on how they can select individuals with experience in these sectors, possess credibility in these

sectors, and develop creative workforce programs to deal with the needs of these sectors because they come out of these sectors.

One barrier I think that will happen is as community colleges want to offer four-year or advanced degrees. That pushes the college away from getting industry-specific skill sets.

We still have a tendency not to see community workforce development as in all aspects of the college. Workforce should be part of all areas—including counseling, theater, and liberal arts. We should develop programs that cut across individual academic subject lines. But having enough money to run program equipment and having faculty who understand the technology are also issues.

Several programs can be done well online, particularly online classes that are useful for incumbent workers who know their industries and know the jobs because they work in those jobs. It is possible to add to their skill sets through online education if these individuals are motivated and already have good foundational skills.

Online education is probably less important to new workers. One example is nursing. Our nursing programs have practicums. People go into hospitals, and they learn what nurses do because they do what nurses do. No online class can substitute for that hands-on experience.

To the degree that online education works in workforce areas, I think I see it as more of an enhancement to incumbent worker training and an enhancement to adults already in the workforce. I see it less as a principal gateway for younger people, people changing careers, or first-time learners.

For individuals who are new Americans, such as new immigrants to the country, online learning must be mediated by classroom work because one fundamental issue that we've seen with new immigrants is the need for them to speak to, and interact with, others.

Online learning plays a role. It also has a certain target audience, and is not for everyone. Many important forms of learning technology have been introduced in the classroom or in the laboratory. Not every program can have enough money to use real-time, real-live equipment. Some simulation packages and some other computer-based technologies have become essential for all students.

According to Blytheville–based Arkansas Northeastern College President James Shemwell:

There are three challenges I would like to talk about. One is obvious—funding. We all know that. One big issue we have with funding here at Arkansas— I don't know whether this is a problem universally in the country, but it is true in many states—is the state has a funding formula. All states do. Arkansas does it based on a university model. What I mean by that is it does not consider the cost of technical education. It assumes everybody is sitting in a classroom, and maybe there is a computer in there or a projector. But that's it.

The cost of equipment and training for some fields is higher than for others. We ask the students to pay for consumable supplies, but there are so many other instructional costs we can't pass on to students because it would simply be too expensive for them. That is a huge problem. Those costs are not factored into the funding formula. When they show statistics that the state is covering a fixed percentage of funding, the number means nothing. It is bogus. That is a funding problem.

Another issue with financing, too, is that community colleges rarely have much political clout. In Arkansas, community colleges do not have the political clout that universities do. We formed a consortium of 22 institutions working together. We stick together because we realize that, with 22 of us in Arkansas, we touch just about every legislator in Arkansas. That is powerful.

A second problem is perception. That is a problem. I will tell you a funny story. It happened last week. I sat down one evening, and my wife was watching something on TV. The movie showed a beautiful home on the ocean. It just fascinated me, and I thought, I wonder what these people do for a living to afford such a nice estate. They were writers! Don't all writers have that lifestyle? It is absurd the professions they show of successful people in popular culture. It gives people the wrong impressions. There is such a staggeringly small percentage of people that succeed as writers. The foils, the people portrayed as unsuccessful, are engaged in manufacturing, service, or retail. These are the losers—or at least that is the message. I am delighted that we see push back because it creates a huge problem of perceptions with young people.

The third issue—and this is probably the biggest barrier we face—is the concept of social promotion. We have got so many students—and I have seen it in my 20 years of college, and it is just accelerating and getting worse. I don't blame our teachers, and I don't blame our local administrators because I think they are working on a system that has done this to them. In many kindergarten through 12th-grade systems, there are no significant consequences for nonperformance.

Prestonsburg, Kentucky–based Big Sandy Community and Technical College President Devin Stephenson reiterates the funding issues raised by so many others:

> For me, the primary barrier in carrying out the leadership role centers on financial resources. I see our institutions already working "lean and mean" and, in fact, we are the most effective and efficient sector of higher education in regard to utilization of our resources. We give the state government that allocates appropriations and the taxpayers the best value for their money when it comes to higher education and workforce training.
>
> I think if we can get all of our legislators and congressional delegations to understand the important role we play and to improve the financial resources that are appropriated to us, we will impact more lives and have a greater impact on the communities we serve. Our challenges are staying ahead of the current technology trend. It is difficult to do that with financial barriers created by declining state appropriations.
>
> Second, finding academic leaders who are entrepreneurial in spirit is critically important. Many individuals earn their terminal degrees, write their dissertations, but when they get on the ground they have a difficult time seeing the forest for the trees. They can't fit the pieces of the puzzle together to

practically apply the theory. I want to teach and inspire our leadership team to think entrepreneurially, innovatively, and creatively. I want them to think about what value they can add and how they can use that value to transform our students, our institution, and our region.

Just last week my maintenance operations director came to me and said he had been thinking about what I had been saying about acting more entrepreneurially. As a result of two retirements in his department, he wants to reorganize our maintenance and operations department to save the institution approximately $50,000 a year. I know now that what I have been saying is getting through and being applied practically. It is tough to find academic leaders who think entrepreneurially and can demonstrate success in connecting their programs externally to the community.

Another challenge is finding people who can communicate effectively with other people. There are many great educators out there, but they have difficulty in communicating both orally and in writing. This multigenerational workforce whom we all serve is extremely challenging when it comes to creating clearly understood lines of communication. We have to learn how to use interpersonal relationships and good communication streams to help fulfill the institution's mission and to "make things happen."

Another challenge we face in regard to communication is that we live in an age of texting and emails. Instead of walking to the office next door or down the hall to deliver a message or solve a problem, we text or email, thus eliminating effective and essential face-to-face dialogue that includes body language and facial expressions that are so important in quality communication. Our society prefers to do that and I think it is a nemesis to collaboration. It leads to an accumulation of miscommunication. I want to build our institution's internal operations organically and that is to be interconnected and alive, exercising "give and take" and problem solving and solution seeking in a lively ecosystem.

According to Moorefield-based Eastern West Virginia Community and Technical College President Charles Terrell:

> As far as obstacles, I see expertise as one. I mean experts within the leadership of community colleges. How do we help with that transitional planning? You referenced another one will always be local politics. How do we rise above politics? How do we assume the facilitator role and bring people together to solve problems?
>
> Human capital is another challenge I see, especially for rural community colleges. Regardless of the size of a community college, many people wear multiple hats. We have heard the same frequently, that colleges are doing more with less. We ask our people if they can take on many additional tasks. We are struggling with that right now because the college is becoming more involved in facilitating economic and community development.
>
> I didn't share that, for our economic development strategy, we have identified several sectors for our region. They include advanced manufacturing (small scale), agricultural (and there are enormous opportunities there), agriculture technology, the food-to-table initiatives (and, because of our proximity

to major metropolitan areas, provide a new pathway for food to table), arts, tourism, and technology.

We struggle because the college has been facilitating this great regional discussion but does not have adequate staff to keep all this energy flowing and keep conversations and partnerships engaged. We have to be careful. The college is perceived as the leader when we bring all these new partners to the college. When we assume that leadership role, there is the responsibility to keep the momentum and see action instead of just having another meeting for the sake of having a meeting. Then people grow discouraged.

I think what we are struggling with now is identifying additional human capital to assist us with these regional community development initiatives.

Now, I like to think of myself as an entrepreneur. I think that is what I would also encourage new community college presidents to do. Remind me to share the effectuation model because I think that will be a wonderful model for new presidents or new leaders to consider.

Getting creative, we are looking now at working with some of our smaller communities successfully in recruiting AmeriCorps volunteers. How can the college seek AmeriCorps volunteers whose task would provide us with additional human capital to keep our regional partners engaged? How do we look at federal and private foundation grants? How do we bring in other resources to drive our regional strategic admissions?

The effectuation model was developed by the National Association for Community College Entrepreneurship. I can send you the reference from the professor at the University of Virginia. Saras Sarasvathy developed this model in her interactions and interviews with successful entrepreneurs. It struck me because it changed my mind-set as a college president. I am actively involved in the NACCE organization. They have a program in which they ask community college presidents to sign a pledge for entrepreneurship. When it first evolved, it was to talk about, or have presidents support, entrepreneurship education. But over the years, this changed with a pledge that the President must think like an entrepreneur and create an entrepreneurial culture within the community college to think differently and look at other resources to help the college fulfill its mission.

The effectuation model starts out with means, a bird in the hand. What do we have? Often we would look at what we want. First, start with *what* because that becomes so important as our foundation. It understands to start with what we can control, what we already have access to. That is our bird in the hand. As we move forward, it is important for an institution to decide what it can afford to lose. Move forward with only that. We don't throw all our chips into the vat. If we lose, it is not good. We're broke, and our institution is in trouble. As we move forward with new initiatives, new partnerships, decide on what we can afford to lose.

The third part we have already talked about. Bring people in as co-creators. Saras refers to it as the crazy quilt. When we look at a quilt we see all those patches. When we start, it is like what is this going to look like, but we have this beautiful outcome. I truly believe in bringing people in as co-creators, and the college because it plays the role of facilitator.

This one is like turning lemons into lemonade. Pivot as changes occur. I love this part because we can't control what happens, but we can control our response. Pivot as we reach certain barriers or reduction in resources. Those things we can't control, but we can control how we respond to it and then how we pivot and look at taking a new direction.

The last one is using a control to drive valuation creation. It is a world-view perspective. A "pilot in the plane" kind of idea. She describes it as control versus prediction. It goes back to the first one. Know what we can control, know what we have access to, and then that drives us into being the pilot of the plane and pivoting as changes occur. That helps the college or institution move forward.

It has become a guiding point for me, and when we started our strategic planning initiative, I shared this effectuation model the first day. If we need it, the institution must know there is a need, and therefore, we address it in our strategic plan. We may not have the funding, but understanding what our needs are provides an important story for us to share with private foundations. It provides critical information when putting together federal and state grants. If we don't know what we need, then it is hard to advocate or share our personal story. That changed their mind-set. They then put down what they have and what they need so we can figure out how we can get from point A to point B.

I will share with you a personal story. I was at a conference. I was in a meeting with a private foundation—there was a group of presidents. Sitting next to me was an entrepreneur who is now our Entrepreneur in Residence. Joe has had a rich history of being a successful entrepreneur. We are listening to this pitch from the private foundation. They announced that they will release a big grant for community colleges. They said it would be $100,000, but when you receive the application, we want to see skin in the game, so we are asking the colleges to match $100,000 to that project.

At that same time, that effectuation model was introduced. What happened is I made the statement that $100,000 would be hard for us to locate, and in eight months we raised $200,000. I totally get it. It changed my mind-set. That is one piece of advice I would give future leaders—don't get locked into that pathway of thinking of dependence on state appropriations. We have to become entrepreneurial, and we have to be better at telling our story. You have a winning formula when you do that by focusing on success.

According to Palatine, Illinois–based William Rainey Harper College President Ken Ender:

> Staffing is part of the challenge. Many meetings are held. If no one is there to carry those ideas to next steps, many efforts die. One challenge is to provide community college resources consistently to ensure follow-up and follow-through. So, as I think about it, the biggest obstacle or barrier for most community-based transformational efforts is, How do you staff it as it's going on? How do you build the plane while flying it?
>
> When information is inadequate, there is always some posturing. The more a community college can position itself as an information provider and a facilitator, the easier it becomes to work successfully through the egos. I have often found that many leaders in the region and community look to the com-

munity college as an asset they know they need to figure out how to leverage ideas. Community and regional leaders have a natural tendency to want to be good partners with the community college President.

According to American Association of Community Colleges Senior Vice President Jen Worth, "Industry partnering and scaling present persistent challenges to community colleges":

Community colleges want and need consistent industry partners. Engagement is a critical component of that persistence. True partnership with industry cannot be limited to outreach from the college when a need arises, but must be deeper and more meaningful, with mutual benefit realized.

Furthermore, when community college workforce developers engage with an industry partner, that engagement must be organized and not redundant. Industry partners will remember the people from the community college that have come to them in the past. Often, multiple college personnel will serve as points of contact with industry partners. To avoid confusion and duplication, those points of contact should be handled in an organized, coordinated way.

Another challenge that community colleges face is the need to focus on employer needs and not just student outcomes. Community college representatives must learn what employers are doing. Representatives should understand employer focus areas, including their priorities, goals, and expectations for the next year and beyond. Community colleges should do their homework as opposed to telling them, "Here's where we are coming from," and telling them their needs. That reflective approach is critical. There should always be a way to revisit the relationship on a recurring basis.

Effective and lasting industry partnering demands more than putting out a joint press release, having the regular monthly and/or quarterly meetings, and having coffee and donuts once a quarter. The relationship must be reviewed consistently, and it's not about just getting together but about promoting well-earned successes. The relationship should also showcase students' stories. It should include constant feedback about the value of the employer's investment to the college; it should include making sure that, as industry needs change, the college is mindful of those needs. The relationship must evolve and mature.

As this happens, all partners will be reinvested. There are diminishing returns if we continue to do the same things. It's no longer interesting or innovative. So, what's on the horizon for employers, and how does the community college adapt? At the end of everything we are not asking the employer to serve us; rather, we are asking the employer or the industry partner to enable us to serve the students better because we want them to be the hiring entities.

The second thing I might say is about scaling. I would tell an incoming leader that, in a highly diversified system like community colleges, it is difficult to scale things. The scope of community colleges encompasses tribal lands and territory colleges; we have urban colleges, and we have large, statewide systems. On the best day at the local level, all partners connected to the community college are perfectly aligned with every economic development organization, every person on the investment board, and every employer in the region. But those days are not that frequent. It's very difficult to find those perfect alignment days.

There's always going to be one new need or one new partner we are trying to engage or one new committee we are trying to attract so we can do new work. And it's ripe because it speaks to the fact that these connections and pertinent challenges are always evolving. When we find a compelling lesson or best practice we think we should share across the field, it is a challenge to apply that lesson to the diversified system.

For a new leader, scaling in a diversified system is difficult. As an example, a leader in downtown Chicago, Illinois, comes upon a phenomenal practice in the use of labor market information. Though all community colleges should use labor market information effectively, the labor market information that a community college gets in downtown Chicago differs from what is available or useful to a community college in Honolulu or the statewide system in Indiana.

The data a community college gets in downtown Chicago is probably perfect because the college is looking at industry needs in Chicago, and they are placed in Chicago. But a community college just outside of Chicago may not find the data or the practice equally useful because it is not specialized to that suburban community or the bedroom community. That new President must still make an assessment and then decide on action. Should the data be used, some of the data, or should the decision be intuitive?

Some community colleges in the Pacific Islands may not have enough data. They can look at all the market information they want, but it may not be enough data or the right data for them to make well-informed decisions. In a statewide system, such as Indiana, looking at one city wouldn't be relevant because there are more than 20 campuses in Indiana, and decision makers must look at it in a more regional or statewide perspective rather than city to city.

Each campus has to use labor market information, but there's a level of sophistication that must be applied when things are not harmonious and perfect in a highly diversified system. New leaders must pay attention to how they apply a best practice to their community colleges. This requires leaders to be skilled craftspersons to see the lesson and modify it to be appropriate to realize the greatest return.

Kenosha, Wisconsin–based Gateway Technical College Vice President of Business and Workforce Solutions Deborah Davidson notes:

> Funding can be a challenge, and I believe it has always been that way. One thing that has changed, and maybe it is all relative, is the cost of equipment. The cost of setting up and operating a nursing lab, a machining lab, or an automotive technician lab is expensive; however, our students need to know the latest technology in order to be prepared for meaningful work. We have cultivated many partnerships with local businesses in order to leverage our state aid while keeping student tuition and fees affordable.
>
> As we meet with employers about their hiring needs we also discuss the types of equipment they require their employees to be trained on. Employer engagement is increasing and they want to know how they can help. They

want to know how they can interact with our students to access them for internships and job placement upon graduation.

Additionally, they are willing to provide us access to their equipment suppliers for equipment purchases or possible donations of equipment, materials, and supplies. Through these types of business partnerships employers get name recognition at our college, their logo in a lab or their name on a partnership wall, or in some cases, their equipment in the classroom or lab. We have a great partnership with Snap-on Tools. Our students experience their quality tools in our automotive, engineering, manufacturing, diesel, horticulture, HVAC, and other programs.

We have established partnerships with businesses to achieve complementary goals. We have jointly developed curriculum with Snap-on, Trane, Starrett, and others. As a college our strength is teaching and learning. We know how to develop curriculum that leads to stated learning outcomes. And the company knows the tools and technology behind their products. By working together, we achieve better results for our students, making them job-ready upon program completion.

Industry partnerships means both the community college and the business partner are engaged. We are working as partners, not as customer and vendor. This has made a big difference in how our labs look. When we put a company's name on our wall, we have a relationship with them. That is their brand and their reputation and we know we have to live up to that. Our labs must always look professional and reflect the professional image of any and all company logos on the wall.

Lakewood, Washington–based Clover Park Technical College Special Assistant to the President Mabel Edmonds observes, "The greatest barrier or challenge is the lack of adequate resources to address the needs that have been identified by colleges and communities. Even though we have been innovative in mobilizing and utilizing the resources we have, there is still much to be done and not enough funding and hours in the day."

Cleveland, Ohio–based Cuyahoga Community College (Tri-C) Executive Vice President of Workforce, Community, and Economic Development William Gary repeats a common theme voiced by so many others:

I believe the chief barrier right now is finance. As you know, most workforce development programs today are self-sustaining. We have to survive based on revenues from enrollments and services provided to businesses and students.

The second barrier is the notion of convincing various community leaders and businesses that community colleges are the solution providers for workforce, community, and economic development. Typically, most businesses, depending on whether they are knowledge-based economies or smokestack economies, often think four-year institutions are the only solution providers because of their research and development capabilities.

Community colleges are the "boots on the ground." And we must communicate better and provide testimonies of our capabilities and results, and get the industries to testify on our behalf—get the industries to begin to put skin in the game by underwriting programs, equipment, and funding these initiatives so that they reap positive and sustainable outcomes. Moreover, we need to get the community-based organizations to understand better the importance of their participation and accountability in this process. Make sure that they have a vested interest in ensuring their constituencies are given every opportunity for education and training.

Another barrier I see is participating in an economic structure where there is no unified and strategic plan for workforce and economic development. In order to be successful, all stakeholders involved in workforce development initiatives must be strategically focused, and governed by a "systems approach plan of strategy" that lays out a comprehensive plan for addressing training, employment, community engagement, and economic development. Community colleges, like Tri-C, can serve as "conveners" in developing and implementing such a strategy.

I've got the commitment from our college President, who wants workforce development as visible and involved as any other program in the college. And that is a key challenge for us in the community college system, to balance workforce with academics and to also get our faculty to understand that the workforce component is not a detriment to the pristine halls of academia. We are a complement to the academic piece and, in some cases, drive enrollments to their programs.

This role also includes acquiring additional funding sources to the college, to include grants, philanthropic funding sources, and programs that are aligned to generate revenue from businesses.

Chapter Six

How Technology Is Changing the Face of Education

The growth of online education is a well-known fact. So too are other applications of technology to education. Annual studies show online education growing everywhere in the United States. Gamification and simulations have also affected education. How will technology affect community colleges? It was a question we posed to the Thought Leaders.

According to Kenosha, Wisconsin–based Gateway Technical College President and Chief Executive Bryan Albrecht:

> I would say that community colleges have been forerunners in online delivery. Thirty percent of all of our courses are delivered online, and another 20 percent are offered in a hybrid model (some online and some on site), and the availability of the unique programs we offer can limit us. Sometimes it is difficult to serve a dental assistant program online because students must gain hands-on experience. It's tough to teach cosmetology students to style or cut hair online because they must have a face-to-face lab.
>
> But there are ways we can build hybrid experiences and simulations into programs. We have many simulations on the computer now, and we see that more of our students have access to computer technology. Our communities have a broadband-based network, and so there's access at home. Online programs will continue to grow, and we support that. We deploy several online programs to area high schools. That seems to be a convenient way to connect community colleges with the high schools, because high schools have different delivery schedules, meaning the bell schedule for classes differs greatly from our own. But we can make it more convenient to connect by offering classes online, because it seems to match their delivery schedule better.

According to Harrisburg, Pennsylvania–based Harrisburg Area Community College President John J. Sygielski:

> I believe technology impacts community colleges in a meaningful and exciting way. How we market our credit or noncredit programs and services within our 10-county service region and beyond is just one of the positive outcomes of using technology. For example, we do mass mailings. When people register by entering a code, the code triggers for us as an identifier of who the individual is and what information he or she may seek.
>
> Another example is a specific zip code can identify for us what part of our service region is interested in taking classes from us so we are better able to target marketing dollars. With all of this information, we will understand the age demographics we need to serve and then partner with a radio station that serves those 18- to 23-year-olds as opposed to other age groups.
>
> Technology has also affected online learning. We now offer 15 online associate degrees serving over 7,000 students who are participating through online and blended (face-to-face and online) coursework, and that's the only area of the college that's increased its enrollment almost every semester since I arrived in 2011. We also train school districts and companies in how to offer their information online by encouraging company representatives in our service region to go through our online training programs so their human resources departments can either contract with us or develop their own training programs for their employees.
>
> The senior leadership team at the college joins me in championing alternative systems of instructional delivery. In fact, HACC has invested significant resources into blended and distance-learning coursework and programs and ensures our faculty and employees are as current as possible through innovative professional development activities facilitated by some of our most innovative faculty. Online and blended learning is not only a critical issue for me as President but for all of us, as it helps us remain current and relevant to address many of the changing learning needs of our students, businesses, and the communities we serve.

According to Charlotte, North Carolina–based Central Piedmont Community College President P. Anthony Zeiss:

> There's no doubt technology is changing the face of education. And I will tell you, here's what's happening. Many services for human development run counter to existing educational structures. In many respects the old university model is rapidly becoming obsolete for many people. Students can take classes on their iPhones or iPads, and many people are. Technology will undoubtedly affect what we do and who we are. Education and training, like other services, will move toward a cloud structure. That means the information will become available to anyone, anytime and anywhere in the world. We [community colleges] have to adjust and ready ourselves for that. Many people are already working on it.
>
> But we face several problems and challenges, the least of which is tradition (that is, we have never done it that way before, or we are not used to that,

or such education cannot be delivered with quality, and so forth). We better get past those self-imposed delusions, or we will find ourselves to be obsolete.

At Central Piedmont Community College, innovation is a core value. We have many online classes, and we measure what we do because we are focused on student success. We look at data. We discovered that students take online classes because they couldn't get the traditional regular scheduled classes. It wasn't the first choice. But that's changing. However, their achievement levels were 40 percent below students enrolled in traditional on-site classes. We no longer teach pure online classes, but we offer many hybrid or blended classes.

We are a leading community college in developing competency-based, self-paced curricula for developmental classes in English, reading, and math. Time becomes an acceptable variable, and students can proceed at their pace. We are excited about that. Fortunately, I led a national experiment in the 1980s on competency-based education in technologies and technical training, and it was a wild success. We were producing ASWA Certified Welders in three and a half months instead of two years. The traditional educators got upset because they feared they would lose their jobs. We have to get beyond that fear and focus on student success and becoming competitive on the world stage.

Larry A. Ferguson, President of Bevill State Community College in Su- miton, Alabama, notes:

> The debate over whether we should offer classes online really doesn't exist anymore. You know that, initially, there was much resistance from faculty in moving classes online. With KCTCS just this past year, we had 30,000-plus online students. What we are finding is that this delivery modality offers many opportunities and strengths. But we must know that we have to ensure there is quality in the delivery of that programming online.
>
> We are getting more requests from our business and industry partners for online education options, but I will say the majority of what they are asking for are blended solutions. One example is a hospital I worked with in northeast Kentucky. They had industrial maintenance folks working 24/7. When there is downtime, they want them to do some online learning work and then at some point connect face-to-face with an instructor to ensure that the quality of learning was there, that they understood, or expand on concepts and principles they need. We are getting the most requests for the blended approach.
>
> As we hire new faculty members, one criterion we look for is experience with, or willingness to understand, the pedagogy of online teaching. Our younger faculty embrace that. I think this is a shift in focus. Online learning is here to stay.

James Shemwell, President of Arkansas Northeastern College in Blythe- ville, reemphasizes the view of others:

> The imperative to reach students through online means is no less for commu- nity colleges than it is for universities. It is not just about online classes. What we as community colleges must do is build better online support mechanisms

for online education. I have seen that evolve during my time here. Believe it or not, I was one of the early pioneers here in online education. It fascinated me.

That was around the turn of the century. It was back when I was Dean for Technical Programs. I heard about the delivery of classes over the Internet, and I wondered how they did that. I investigated it. I had a faculty member in my area; she was interested in it and said she would like to try it. I encouraged it. Online learning grew from there. But for so long when we talked about online here at our college, we were talking about online classes.

There was a huge pushback. How do we know students aren't cheating? How do we know somebody else isn't doing their work? We had much pushback. The effect of that pushback has diminished. It has gotten much better because we addressed the issues. When faculty members see their contemporaries use it, then they concede that they should look at it. But initially there was tremendous resistance.

As we progressed, all conversations focused on how to deliver the classes. We needed to have conversations, and we had those on how we advise online students. How do they apply online? How do they apply for financial aid online? How do they pay their bills online? These questions, and many others, also came up.

We offered online classes for at least 10 years before students could apply for financial aid online and before they could pay bills online. That is recent. For the longest time we did not truly have online students. We had residential students who could take classes online.

The way I became Dean is an interesting story. I mentioned I was an off-campus manager at one of our satellite campuses. The Solutions Group exploded. The idea worked. It got bigger, and it took most of my time managing our customized training operation. The person who had been Dean of our business and technical programs left and took a job elsewhere. Our CAO said he would promote me but wanted to marry two areas. It was very innovative. I give him credit. We married noncredit customized training with for-credit traditional programs. It was a great marriage.

We realized that most of what we were doing in customized programs was worthy of credit. It was just not delivered on Mondays and Wednesdays, and it doesn't look like a college schedule. But these are college educations we are delivering. We built credit courses on the customized side and then on the traditional side we saw issues more from an employer perspective. Putting those two areas together was a wise move, and the CAO gets all the credit for that.

We are working to develop human capital. We are working with students. Eventually students will work somewhere. Employers are not just large companies. In some of our programs, the advisory councils we form are comprised of small business people. They are entrepreneurs. They give us advice because some of our future students we hope will become entrepreneurs. Some have done that.

According to Devin Stephenson, President of Big Sandy Community and Technical College in Prestonsburg, Kentucky:

Technology is affecting us in a major way. I will give you an example. Today, 30 percent of our credit hours are created through online platforms. That seems to be the way of life now, and I believe it will be the way of the future. I am currently looking at an administrative reorganization of the college that establishes a dean over our virtual campus. I believe we should pay attention to how learners learn and interact and to how they perceive educational delivery. Not everyone is capable and effective at online learning, but some will take one or two courses and then become strong advocates and will want the online format so they can continue to work full-time.

This impacts us organizationally, because schools have not adequately adjusted personnel and resources toward the shift in online learning. We have to create a college without walls. We must create it and do it right now if we want to succeed.

Technology will also force our faculty and staff to be more engaging with students. We have always believed faculty members are performers. The classroom is a stage. But students are getting information much faster than we have ever seen and attention spans are much shorter. Student engagement will be critical and our faculty cannot teach as they have taught in the past.

We must touch the learning styles—the visual, the auditory, and the high-touch learner. Technology will drive how we do business. I am not saying it is the best thing. I am evaluating it now, but it is driving the way we do business to be more efficient and more effective. Of course, demand will determine how we provide the supply. If we are going to be successful, then we must respond to those demands.

But Charles Terrell, President of Eastern West Virginia Community and Technical College in Moorefield, sounds caution:

We have to keep it blended. We can't rely on an online format, because, from my perspective—and maybe I'm a little old-school—but I still see the value of face-to-face interactions. I see great value in flexible learning spaces. We are now taking the initiative here with our traditional learning spaces and turning them into collaborative learning spaces where faculty can ask the students to get up and move the table and chairs around to form work groups.

Some classes are not designed to do that. When you get into computer labs where we are now going to laptops—touchscreen laptops—on mobile carts. That way the faculty member can walk into a classroom and organize a group session. Then the next half of the class the faculty member can invite students to go over to the cart, grab their computers, and work on some project. It is blended delivery.

Broadband is critical because it provides access to information and disseminates information for telecommuters. From an economic development strategy, technology can be important because, in our geographic area, we are looking at how can we provide skills to our students to be competitive to apply for jobs that will enable them to work here in West Virginia, but to work with a federal agency and stay off the Beltway in D.C.

My recommendation is to blend delivery. We still need the traditional learning methods. We have already been talking about how do we facilitate discussions and for that you can use technology. But much of it should be face-to-face interaction. Going online will work for some students, but when you look at the majority of students in a rural community lacking skills—and sometimes they lack the self-confidence—that can be a very dangerous gamble, to make a 100 percent investment in an online curriculum.

According to Palatine, Illinois–based William Rainey Harper College President Ken Ender:

> Some people see this as a threat; others see it as an opportunity. Technology has the potential of delivering education as a commodity. To many, that is a scary thought because the word "transaction" seems so independent of people. If you think about technology as the medium, content is the outcome. If I am a faculty member or if I am a president that has been in the business for 40-some-odd years, the question is, Where does the institution go? Where will we find our role? We will find that using technology will provide us a better capacity to customize the work we do for individual learners and better coach people to achieve desired outcomes. The faculty's role becomes more that of a facilitator/coach and technology provides the medium for transmitting information.
>
> Frankly, if you think about the scale on which we need to operate our country around the delivery of postsecondary credentials, the person-driven model we have is scalable to maybe 20 percent of a nation. There was a time when that was all we needed. But in an era when 80 percent of folks need some postsecondary education, a person-driven medium based in a classroom does not work. The questions become (1) how do we use technology to build a customized approach for each student? and (2) how do we use faculty expertise to become better transmitters of information and coaches to individuals experiencing difficulty? I believe that is coming. Some faculty members are already doing it. However, they are at the early stages of such an educational delivery system.
>
> The sweet spot for most students will be blended online instruction where we have a mixture of face-to-face and online learning. We see more adult and younger students taking online courses. They like the convenience. We see many students taking one or two online courses to help them with their schedule around work. As students become more comfortable with the tablet tool, we expect an increase in blended online instruction. Most of our students in school have tablets now. The next generation is pushing us into using technology more as a medium of instruction.

Jen Worth, American Association of Community Colleges Senior Vice President, offers a most helpful perspective:

> In order to address this question, we need to go through *how we teach*, *what we teach*, and *what we teach on*.
>
> There are more models now of students doing collaborative or communal learning with fast risk-taking. Those models have to be taught in the ways in which they will be used in the workplace. This applies whether you say you

believe in hybrid or blended learning or face-to-face and/or all online. I'm talking about something that I've learned from Dave Garza at Querium.

He explains that, in the IT sector, people are expected to do coding projects. What might happen is that Annie might work in Kentucky, and she might have to write code in a collaborative, fast-paced way with a person in Shanghai and a person in Sydney, Australia. The three must carry out that project quickly, and then they will have to route it back and give it to each other. The project may then cycle back to their employer, sitting in New York.

They won't be doing just one project in a week; rather, they will do four or five other projects simultaneously. Annie may have to work with Mike, Bill, and Frank on something else. Or another network of five to 10 people someplace else. That work situation differs radically from sitting in a classroom or online setting where students work on one assignment with a singular focus or by themselves and then turn the results in at the end of the week.

We need to know that we are teaching our students in environments that reflect, realistically, where they will have to apply their skills. This requires us to think differently about how we ask our students to show us what they know. It also requires that we teach in an environment that allows us to test our students and to teach them and to replicate their learning like that work environment. While that may be a real IT example, there are other, comparable sectoral examples.

In the health care space I've seen some exceptional teaching and learning models at different community colleges around the country. In the nursing programs, they use people of varying ages and sizes to create a mock emergency room, and the nursing students get to experience that. The faculty members can insert disaster scenarios and have different applied-learning opportunities that make sense and are relevant.

I've also seen community colleges where whole cities have been built with actual firehouses and police stations so students can crash cars and observe as Emergency Medical Technicians [EMTs] or first responders cut the car in half and pull out the "victims." The EMTs work on those victims while other students take the "drunk drivers" away to the police station. They then process those individuals through the court system where there's a legal student preparing the case.

Everything is filmed, and students are given workshops on the lessons learned for the next iteration of coursework. There's process improvement. The courses are integrated because everything happens in real time just as it does in the real world. The EMTs would work with the police, while the police are simultaneously feeding into the court system. To pretend that our classroom work occurs in isolation isn't sufficient anymore.

We need real-world simulations that show actual integration and cross-pollination. This is also true in courses like entrepreneurship. The key is to teach small business courses and not teach those courses in isolation but integrate the application of skills. In one community college, they wanted to teach viticulture and wine making. Because bottles are not made to sit on the shelves but to be sold, programs should be teaching students great wine making and also how to make their businesses stronger.

How we teach needs to change. I gave you the coding example initially because that was a specific example of technology. In integrated programs—

like the model of the car crash in the city model, and the first responders—
technology is helping us. It allows us to look, almost from an aerial view, at
the areas of progression between the different departments: how they integrate
and how we teach our students to internalize how all these instances connect to
the whole situation. This moves students from pure knowledge to applied
knowledge.

Technology is our newest form of literacy. It doesn't matter what particular sector we are talking about; it could be designing apps for a phone, it could
be health care, engineering, commercializing a product, or 3-D modeling activities. It can even be fields like politics. Technology no longer stands alone
and is required for every student to acquire not only digital literacy but pro-
gressive technical literacy. If we are to educate an incoming president, vice
president, or the deans and the chairs—or any leadership executive position for
workforce and economic development—we need to expect as much from our
students as we expect from ourselves.

It's important for us to make certain that our students have ready, reliable
access and that they are pushing themselves. As a teaching team, we must
engage with more collaborative, and fast-paced, models ourselves.

Teaching platforms have changed. In the past, VHS tapes and subsequent-
ly DVDs were used. They could be exchanged and it worked. Technology
progressed to online classes where students would watch instructors. There
was vibrant discussion about whether learning should be synchronous or asyn-
chronous and whether we should do it independently or collaboratively. From
there, we progressed to handheld devices.

Now there are many platforms. Phones are ubiquitous. However, with the
variations come a confusing number of different vendors serving higher education. It becomes tricky for community college executives to make smart
choices as they try to discern which vendors are in it for the right reasons. In
the technology space, it's very important for leadership to listen with two ears.
With one ear: *What technology will help our community college to become
more effective as a business in its own right?* With the other ear: *What will
help the college to create a cultural partnership that will be the fundamental
building block for our professional staff and students?* A technology partner or
vendor should want to help them think about how they can ensure that their
teaching and what they teach in the technology space is most current and
cutting-edge. It is not so much a vendor relationship as it should be a true
partnership.

**Gateway Technical College Vice President of Business and Workforce
Solutions Deborah Davidson of Kenosha, Wisconsin, notes:**

Gateway is a technical college and as such we have always had an applied,
hands-on approach to teaching. We have some online programs at the college
in accounting, business management, and graphic communications. We use
Blackboard technology for most of our college courses integrating a blended
approach.

Some colleges have moved to open labs staffed by faculty. Student learn
through online modules and activities and then go into the open lab to practice,

apply, and be assessed for mastery of content. I think this approach has some validity; however, we do not have this model in place at Gateway at this time.

Mabel Edmonds, Special Assistant to the President at Clover Park Technical College in Lakewood, Washington, explains that "technology is a wonderful asset and is envisioned to be an even greater resource in the future; however, some people want face-to-face engagement, want to visit campus, and others want to participate in experiences that are less personal via technology. Colleges will need to be creative in how they meet the needs of the diverse populations served."

On an upbeat note, Cuyahoga Community College Executive Vice President of Workforce, Community, and Economic Development William Gary of Cleveland, Ohio, observes that

> technology is changing education in a positive way. Use of technology is key to enhancing one's workforce readiness for almost every industry sector seeking qualified and skilled workers. In addition, we're expanding our use of technology as a training modality via online learning as a means of student access. So we've been building programs here that are adaptable to this technological modality.
>
> The other thing that is now surfacing in Cleveland is the demand from business for online training for incumbent workers. So we have what we call a Corporate College that is solely designed to provide corporate contract and customized training utilizing both online and brick-and-mortar training. So our online training is a key component and strategy for our workforce development initiatives. Lean Six Sigma leadership training is very big here, and we are using online modalities for that purpose. We are taking, by the way, our CNC machining and welding programs and adapting these to online scenarios. We are even building mobile lounges to house manufacturing equipment and processes to take on site to high schools and business sites where that type of training can be exported to those particular sites.

Chapter Seven

The Community College President's Role in Workforce Development

A leader always sets the tone for an organization. For that reason, we asked the Thought Leaders what role they believe the community college President should play in workforce development.

Bryan Albrecht, Gateway Technical College President and Chief Executive in Kenosha, Wisconsin, observed that

the community college President must be the champion for our community. He or she helps to shape the vision of why the community college exists and what value it plays in workforce development strategy. By saying that, I mean he or she must spend time in the community to understand the community's needs. I serve on 60 boards. I am very active in the community, and I believe that helps me to take the community's pulse.

However, not everything is driven by the workforce. I am on many community committees that allow me to do strategic planning and look at community development, foundation development, school district planning and development, and all those eventually will affect Gateway and workforce training. If the President does not remain active in community boards and committee work, he or she will find it hard to know all elements of what will make a community successful. People have their own unique priorities. My job is to connect those priorities with what Gateway can offer as services and become part of the solution for our community.

We must emphasize that some students just want to sign up because they want to go to college. But we need to find out how Gateway can be a solution provider for our community. And that might well be workforce training, customization of that, or it might be workforce development or broadband initiatives within our community. And there are many ways we can become service providers. That may be a nontraditional view of the community college President role, but for me it's been something that I believe helps to create visibility for our campus.

Even though we are 104 years old this year, many people have not heard about us or have not recently been on campus. We have a new generation of community citizens who have gotten an impression of Gateway from one or two classes. But my job as President is to sell the entire Gateway package. The President connects community college resources to the community and must find more ways to build community connections.

Central Piedmont Community College President P. Anthony Zeiss of Charlotte, North Carolina, emphasized how important is the tone set by the President:

Presidents should shape the culture for their institution and set the tone. They should formulate a vision for their institutions. They should participate in creating a vision for their community and their region. They should lead the college and the community to new heights of student and community success. It's all about student and community success.

Presidents should be key leaders in workforce and economic development. Community colleges have become the economic development engines of our nation. The President must be a principal leader and play a crucial role in the economic development of his or her region.

I spoke at an international workforce conference in Zurich last year. Only two Americans spoke: Jill Biden and me. I was so impressed with her. She was our commencement speaker in 2015. I spoke in Spain in June 2015 at another international workforce development conference. It's great, and it is fun. Many educators in other nations do not understand how to develop training programs like American community colleges because they have the upper class and the lower class, and no middle class. They realize that, clinically and socially, they have to develop a middle class. That's what made the United States great after World War II.

Bevill State Community College President Larry A. Ferguson of Sumiton, Alabama, opined that this

is a superb issue to raise. [The President's role] has evolved over the past few years. The President of the college must take a commanding, leading role in workforce and economic development because community colleges often are the source for workforce development in rural communities. Community colleges are leaders in providing workforce development leading to economic development. So it is critical that the President is highly engaged, involved in all those activities within the community. Presidents should create collaborative, active working relationships with the superintendents of the secondary schools. Education is a continuum, and all parts are critical.

The President should serve on the local board for economic development, whatever it is. That president should assist if the state is involved in activities like creating work-ready communities. I am sure you probably heard of that initiative. We have examples in Kentucky where several presidents helped to lead that initiative within their communities and to certify that their community is "work ready." That makes a difference when those small communities are looking to recruit businesses from around the world.

The President plays an enormous role in workforce and economic development. The issue recently is not just about educational access, although it is still that. The community college also provides the link to support the economic activity within your region. It is all about economics.

Some folks don't like to hear that, and presidents might disagree with what I just said. But what we see now is that the presidents are making these things happen—and I will categorize those again as entrepreneurial leaders—to think differently. They think almost like businesspeople in asking how they capitalize on the resources they have to better their communities, their local businesses, and the individuals they serve by providing education.

"We, as leaders, have to set the example as visibly engaged and successful collaborators," noted Big Sandy Community and Technical College President Devin Stephenson of Prestonsburg, Kentucky:

When I first came to this institution, I met with my leadership team and laid out what I believed defined a successful organization and what attributes a successful leader should possess. One of those attributes was to be a visibly engaged leader and collaborator.

I think to succeed in workforce development the President must be a contributor. The President cannot sit on the sidelines; the President cannot delegate leadership to someone else because the community leaders and influencers want to know the President of the institution is as committed to institutional success as the CEOs of industry and business are to the success of their organizations. Involvement is critical for the President and I believe the President's role is to open the spaces, create opportunities, and then empower people to put the pieces of the puzzles together and make things happen.

Becoming part of the Chamber of Commerce Board is what I have found to be critically important when I move into a community. Last night I was inducted into the Southeast Kentucky Chamber of Commerce Board. The minute I found out that I was appointed to this position [President of Big Sandy Community and Technical College], I called the Chamber Director and I contacted the Executive Director of SOAR [Shaping Our Appalachian Region], and I told both of them I wanted to be an integral part of what their organizations are doing in transforming the region.

Fortunately, both were accepting of my offer to partner and collaborate and now I find myself visibly engaged at the Chamber level on economic development boards, working with industry officials and as the Kentucky Community and Technical College System Liaison to SOAR. However, I am confident that our active engagement with both organizations would not have taken place unless I had proactively reached out and expressed my passion for contributing to the solution. The important role we play is to be a visually engaged partner and a successful collaborator.

Another major challenge for leaders in today's community and technical college sector is environmental assessment and the monitoring of whether or not an institution's services and programs are relevant. If a president doesn't work diligently at it, the institution can easily become ineffective. The new normal is an environment of change, and leaders who can adeptly lead a change culture and manage change will be successful.

You cannot spend a great deal of time looking backward, but you must focus the majority of your time facing forward—in the direction you are leading the organization. I often say, "If you get stuck in tradition, you will be history." During my career I have spent much time working with community leaders, government officials, and influencers to connect the college's resources to the future. That is where hope, promise, and possibility are abundant.

Palatine, Illinois–based William Rainey Harper College President Ken Ender stresses the role of the community college President as a facilitator of sorts:

Often we [community colleges] are viewed as a community asset without an agenda. We are a neutral voice. We have convening capacity. I think that's one role that presidents can take up uniquely. I think "convening and championing" are the two Cs that I'd include in this role. It is a unique role in many communities to have an institution positioned to reach across, down, and up to bring together all interested stakeholders in the community, economic, and workforce development process.

Let me provide an example. Our Learn and Earn program was unique. It was not always there. We developed it with all the characteristics to attract the stakeholders to the table. My instinct about leadership is that, if we bring the interested parties to the table and provide them with all the same information so that all are working from the same scorecard, we will get much better solutions than any one group could accomplish alone.

Using our convening role, we organized a daylong summit on manufacturing and assembled leaders of businesses, secondary and postsecondary schools, and economic development in our region. We spent a day examining the issues affecting the supply-side-of-labor challenge for these manufacturers. We came out of that event with a clear vision we needed to establish proactive ways to drive the talent pipeline. It took about a year to put together a solution—about 12 or 13 of us developing a curriculum based on the competencies developed by the National Manufacturing Association. Eventually, we devised a clear pathway through certifications that resulted in a degree. We then used that to apply for a grant to diffuse the curriculum statewide to a network of other community colleges to encourage them to go through similar activities in their communities. It worked out well.

Lakewood, Washington–based Clover Park Technical College Special Assistant to the President Mabel Edmonds regards the President's role as that of active agent in the community: "Community college presidents should provide leadership within their colleges and their communities. They should be visible and actively engaged—at the planning tables, with business/industry/labor, community-based organizations—and provide suggestions, problem solving, and advocacy for the students served, and identify ways colleges can be more effective, efficient, and relevant in the community. Presidents must set the example, as the educational leaders of their institutions and institutional partners within their communities. If they are to make a difference, the suggestions outlined above will assist them with the desired outcome of being successful."

Chapter Eight

The Community College Dean's Role in Workforce Development

Community college leadership extends beyond the President, of course. For that reason, we asked Thought Leaders about the role of deans in community colleges. They offered a range of perspectives.

Kenosha, Wisconsin–based Gateway Technical College President and Chief Executive Bryan Albrecht emphasizes the Dean's role as an extension of the community college President. As he observes:

> The role of Dean is critical because a Dean is the President's eyes and ears on the campus. I'm all over. I'm in the community, in national events, and on campus. I try to connect the dots where we can, but the real efforts to connect the dots take place at the Dean level. Deans must be careful in carrying out those connections.
>
> The deans help facilitate local improvement. Their workings with the people in the community and employers bring those best practices back to the classroom. They make sure we have the right faculty in the right place, updating curriculum and just being there to support innovative classrooms and labs. They are the strategic building blocks of the strategic vision.
>
> It's one thing to be on the rooftop looking out as the President, meaning seeing the future over the horizon. The executive level is the foundation to make it all happen. But the Dean is the building block that provides the vision to make us look beyond where we are today. We are in a people business; let no one tell you differently. Our job is to connect people. If we can engage people, just like in a classroom if we can engage students, they will succeed. If staff members are engaged and see how they are connected to the bigger picture, they will do extraordinary work.
>
> I'm fortunate to have been appointed to roles on different committee boards. But most of the time, I either reappoint a dean or take a dean with me.

81

Our deans are very active because they know in their own way where I would go with a decision. I don't decide for them, but they know to ask, "Here's the expectations Dr. Albrecht would have; now how can I rally our team to make that happen?"

Harrisburg, Pennsylvania–based Harrisburg Area Community College President John J. Sygielski also stresses the role of the community college Dean in workforce development as that of facilitator:

Five years ago when I arrived, I inherited a variety of unfortunate external and internal issues (for example, $12 million budget deficit, embezzlement allegations, etc.). With this and other issues facing the institution, we significantly realigned the institution.

For example, we opened up all of the Dean positions and rewrote their job descriptions. In those job descriptions, we included the need for them to be involved with our business community. Therefore, it's now a requirement that all deans be actively engaged in advisory committees to ensure they are current and provide the necessary information to inform and impact our credit and noncredit curriculum.

In fact, many of our deans facilitate focus groups in the industries their units represent, such as health care and manufacturing. The focus groups include CEOs and HR directors and are geared to understanding industry training needs, for, as you know, we need to stay very close to the ever-changing needs of our clients and tailor our credit and noncredit accordingly to remain the "first choice for a quality and accessible higher educational opportunity." Our faculty and deans are also engaged in looking at providing prior learning assessments to ensure individuals, especially those in the military, are given credit for demonstrated competencies.

Charlotte, North Carolina–based Central Piedmont Community College President P. Anthony Zeiss stresses the desired autonomy of deans:

Deans should become more like chief operating officers because the President is so busy raising money and working on community initiatives like the Global Vision. Presidents cannot do all of the detailed work as they did in the past.

If faculty members volunteer for workforce development initiatives, and it makes sense for them to be involved, involve them. But don't force them to be involved, because forcing involvement does not work.

Larry A. Ferguson, Sumiton, Alabama–based Bevill State Community College President, indicates that

deans play a critical role. It is those deans, especially in your technical and career areas, that must have a relationship with and understanding of the business and industry in the area.

Many community colleges have advisory boards. When you dig down, however, there are often issues—I call it STP—the *same ten people* (STP) show up at that meeting for 10 years. They meet infrequently. There isn't any quantitative or qualitative discussion on how to improve the curriculum.

I think that is where your Dean must take that leadership for those programs to ensure that we are getting the best feedback needed from business and industry to meet program needs. I am sure you know they are reluctant to do that. Doing that forces deans outside the comfort zone of the college. But they must do that.

When we talk about relationship management in business and industry, it's not just the responsibility of the President but also deans. That is why we are moving toward having customer relationship management tools. If I get a call from a plant somewhere within the state, I can quickly look at the tool to see who is talking with this company, what services have we been providing, and where we stand. That is valuable business intelligence to make sure we can meet their needs.

The relationship management piece of it is not just about shaking hands or hosting lunches; it is about having a strategic approach to those relationships and making sure that we are getting a two-way flow of communication.

Warren, Michigan–based Macomb Community College President James Jacobs supports the views of other Thought Leaders in emphasizing the importance of entrepreneurship among deans:

Community college deans, like other mid-level managers, can't just be administrative pencil pushers where they take Perkins Act money and fill out the right forms. They have to develop themselves as leaders and visionaries.

Part of that is understanding the needs of their community, identifying what skill sets are necessary, and dealing with companies and their needs. Unfortunately, for many reasons which we don't have time to get into, most community college workforce deans tend not to do those things. They are more administrative and make sure that their desk is clean as opposed to seeing themselves more as leaders. The compliance aspect of the job gets overrated, and the visionary part of the job underrated. Unfortunately, scant attention in community college leadership programs is paid to this issue. There are two organizations—professional growth organizations—for community college deans, but the state of leadership and vision is not as high as it should be.

President Devin Stephenson of Prestonsburg, Kentucky–based Big Sandy Community and Technical College stresses the technical and managerial side of the Dean's role in workforce development:

I believe community college deans play the technician/management role in workforce development. Of course, the President should play the visioning/ leadership role. As a president, it is my role to "open the space," and the deans' role to fill up that space. I believe in holding them accountable for that. Deans should both create and implement programs/services and leverage the college's resources for delivery of the programs/services. It is this role that is so important to the overall workforce development delivery system.

Furthermore, the Dean's role must be guided by the words "responsive" and "understanding." If deans don't understand the impact of following through and doing so on a timely basis, and if they are not responsive, then a planned initiative can fail. In developing leadership, I often use the analogy of the flight plan of a pilot. The pilot must be successful at taking off, staying on course, and finally landing the airplane. And so it is with administrators: successfully executing only part of the journey will result in a failed effort. College leaders must be proficient at "landing the airplane" or projects will fail, relationships will end, and institutions will become ineffective.

According to Moorefield–based Eastern West Virginia Community and Technical College President Charles Terrell, deans should help leverage the presence of the President:

> I think they [deans] definitely should be involved. When we look at our large meetings that facilitate economic development and business and industry partners and other service organizations, I am not the only one sitting at the table from the college. It includes our Dean for Career and Technical and Workforce Education. It includes our Director of Workforce. We have a transformational leader through a big federal grant whom we include. It includes other important leaders of the institution, and that is important because they learn about the culture of the institution. Therefore, it worked out great.
>
> There was a recent meeting where I had double-booked. We had probably 30 to 40 people coming to this consortium meeting, and I was scheduled to be in Charleston (our capital). I asked our transformational leader to lead the meeting. She did an excellent job. They probably didn't even miss me.
>
> To answer that question, keeping them engaged provides that transitional planning for leadership. It fits the culture for what everyone at the college knows is the expectation in working with our external stakeholders.

Palatine, Illinois–based William Rainey Harper College President Ken Ender sees deans as content experts in their areas of responsibility:

> When we get down to curriculum development and development of new pathways, we look at the deans as the content experts on behalf of their faculty. Occasionally the Dean has a broad portfolio. We encourage the Dean to involve key faculty so everyone works together.
>
> Deans must put programs together and implement them. I don't want to hand a dean a project; I want the Dean to help build the project with his or her intellectual capital and make a professional investment in the project. Deans are vital to have at the table, and they sponsor much work that gets done. Community college presidents should get people to the table and keep them there. But deans facilitate the work at the table with the faculty.
>
> I don't think funding is growing. That is a challenge. But we can improve how we leverage existing money and connect pools of community assets. That's another reason we cannot think about accomplishing efforts by our-

selves. We have to connect with other resources and other institutions. I have never thought that money was a good reason to say we couldn't do something. I never think too much about where the money will come from. Good ideas find money or that money finds good ideas.

Kenosha, Wisconsin–based Gateway Technical College Vice President of Business and Workforce Solutions Deborah Davidson explains how deans fit into the structure at her institution:

> At Gateway we have academic deans in the following areas: Business and Information Technology; General Studies; Allied Health; Nursing; Manufacturing, Engineering and Transportation; and Service Occupations. Each of our comprehensive campuses (Racine, Kenosha, and Elkhorn) has a Campus who is also a Program Dean. Each of the communities we serve differs from the others (urban/rural, etc.), and the Campus Dean handles the activities of that campus and some of the engagement opportunities in the local community.
>
> In Business and Workforce Solutions, we have an Operations Director, who sits on the Dean's Council and interacts with the deans on a number of faculty-related topics. Additionally, our division collaborates with our academic deans to act on information we gather from companies. Although we have some dedicated faculty in our division, we also utilize academic faculty to meet the needs of employers for customized training, et cetera. Together we are able to respond to the customer in a timely manner and represent the full scope of the college's programs and services for employers.
>
> As is typical when the economy is not doing well, college enrollments increase and contract training with companies decreases due to companies laying off people, or cutting training budgets. We just came through this period and now that employment is up, college enrollments have decreased due to more people working and perhaps taking fewer credits per semester. Contract training has increased due to increased hiring and skill upgrades identified as training needs. Because of our relationship with the program deans, we are able to utilize their faculty for contract training opportunities. This provides a number of benefits to the college, the faculty, and industry. The college is able to provide a full workload for the faculty member while meeting the needs of our customers. The faculty have an opportunity to train in industry, which increases their industry experience and adds to lessons they bring back to the classroom.

Lakewood, Washington–based Clover Park Technical College Special Assistant to the President Mabel Edmonds likens the roles of deans to those of presidents: "Deans have a role similar to their presidents. However, they are key to helping their faculty understand the college's role in workforce development, no matter the program/subject taught. They are all educating/training the workforce for today and the future. Deans and their faculty should learn, plan, and work together for each to be successful in achieving the goals of the college, addressing the needs of students served, and supplying business/industry with the employees needed."

Cleveland, Ohio–based Cuyahoga Community College Executive Vice President of Workforce, Community, and Economic Development William Gary explains the roles of deans based on what they do at his institution:

> Academic deans should play an integral and visible role in workforce development programming and planning. And let me share with you what we are doing to make that happen. We have now created six "Centers of Excellence." The purpose of these centers (Manufacturing; Hospitality Management; Construction/Building Trades; Public Safety; Information Technology; and Nursing/Health Care) is to merge workforce training programs with academic programs to provide pathways that result in multiple options for student success.
>
> These six Centers of Excellence have dual governance structures that include leadership from both workforce development and academic deans' positions. For example, our Manufacturing Center of Excellence is headed by our academic Dean of Engineering as well as our Vice President of Manufacturing, who represents our Workforce Division. Together, they are creating curriculum, meta-majors, and pathways for students that are part of a "One Door, Many Options for Success" strategy that provides students with pathways based on the student's own interests and abilities, choosing the pathways for workforce or for a degree or certification.
>
> Both the deans and the VPs of workforce are working together to make that happen. Did this happen overnight? Absolutely not! There were numerous challenges and obstacles to overcome. First, there was the issue of accreditation: Will combining programs affect accreditation; will students be granted credit for workforce training completed? Will such a "paradigm shift" weaken "academic rigor" or compete with credit program enrollments? We suggest this is not the case—that such a "paradigm shift" adds value to the college mission of student access, student retention, and student success.
>
> To further reinforce the "value add" proposition, I tell our deans that we've been dealing with workforce development in community colleges for over 60 years. But we just didn't label it "workforce"! We simply didn't call it that. Community colleges have been preparing people for the workforce for years. So what makes you think that, when they come and take English and math, they are not preparing themselves for the workforce or a job? So that's the challenge we are facing, and this "paradigm shift" of engaging academic deans is our response.

Chapter Nine

The Community College Faculty Member's Role in Workforce Development

We also wanted to explore the role of faculty members in workforce development. Accordingly, we asked Thought Leaders what they believe the role of faculty members should be.

Sumiton, Alabama–based Bevill State Community College President Larry A. Ferguson emphasized how important it is for faculty members to be current in their fields:

> With faculty we have to often convince them they need to be at the cutting edge of their fields. If they're not on the cutting edge, their students will not have a meaningful credential when they graduate. For many, we see and hear the reluctance until we get them into a session.
>
> We recently facilitated a two-week session at Toyota. We had instructors both from the secondary schools and from our colleges immersed in advanced manufacturing. They loved it. But at first many said they didn't want to give up two weeks of the summer for it. We compensate them. But even then we get resistance.
>
> But, ideally, once they are exposed to professional development, the energy is so intense they don't want to be left behind. They find out that they can't keep teaching industrial maintenance classes unless they know what new issues the instructors are talking about. I think it is a cultural thing. Create a culture where learning is part of what adjunct and full-time faculty are expected to do. So we must build the right expectations. Most build that into the annual performance evaluation piece for faculty. We ask what they have done this year to ensure that they're on the cutting edge.

Ferguson's view was reemphasized by Warren, Michigan–based Macomb Community College President James Jacobs:

On the faculty level, there is a whole issue here about how much faculty are up-to-date. It is one reason part-time faculty members are far more desirable than full-time faculty. They are in the industry. That isn't to say full-time faculty can't keep up or keep ties—but that is too often the case.

Second, what is paramount with full-time faculty is that local industry gets to know the full-time faculty so they become the validator of student skill sets. Often a good faculty member becomes well respected by the company. The great advantage of a community college is it tends not to be exploited. If you have been a good community college in your community for several years, many people doing the hiring in these companies are graduates of your programs.

In developing ties with the alumni, we discovered we have 140,000 alumni. Do we have an alumni organization of 140,000 people? No. But that is our vision. Our vision is to organize the alumni into the sectors they came from. We have a vet-tech alumni group for veterinary technology. We have a designer group that people identify as a community college from the occupational skills they learn. Does it take time and effort and resources to put together these alumni groups? You bet. It also takes invention, and it takes enormous work by deans, associate deans, and others. There is no shortcut for that. We have to spend resources and time.

I want to get to one more critical point. There are too many occupational programs taught by community colleges. If you add the number of programs that an average community college has, they will range between 60 and 200. There is no way any community college can perform all those programs well. Most are only there to provide "an option for students." I think you will see many programs eliminated and consolidated into larger, better programs and look for ways in which cyber (six or maybe 10 at the most) programs are distinctive, are great, are important, and go with them. I think you will see more of that happening. We cannot be all things to all people. We spread ourselves way too thin if we try.

The trick is how you move in that direction given the present staff. Any time you try to close a program or adapt a program, there is always resistance. We need to get out of certain kinds of programs we don't do well. That is where sharing resources comes in, trying to see how community colleges can divide up programs and figure out some we don't do well. That is difficult to do because most community colleges would suffer from declining enrollment.

Prestonsburg, Kentucky–based Big Sandy Community and Technical College President Devin Stephenson emphasizes the importance of faculty in working with students:

I look at faculty members as those on the front line. I think they are central to our mission and extremely important. As a community college leader, I understand how important teaching and learning are to our mission. We are not driven by research or publishing like faculty at four-year institutions. I respect our professors and I respect all of the research going on, but our faculty members are focused on finding that teachable moment. I think their responsibility must be developing a quality learning environment for students and continually being cognizant of our focus on student success.

In workforce development, the focus is on the core subject. In workforce development it isn't so much about the general education component. It is about focusing on filling the skills gaps in a specific skill or trade area. Oftentimes, academic leaders have a difficult time relating to that concept. Some want workforce development programs to have a strong liberal arts focus, when, in fact, business and industry is demanding just the opposite.

Also, the faculty must develop the curriculum in concert with business and industry needs. If they are delivering it they have to understand what industry needs, what part of the curriculum is most relevant, and how to keep it on the cutting edge.

In an early *Star Wars* movie, there was a scene with Yoda and Luke Skywalker where Luke was seeking wisdom from Yoda. I remember Luke telling Yoda he would "try," to which Yoda responded, "No! Try not! Do or do not. There is no try." I have attempted to push the word "try" out of my vocabulary. Our institution will either do it, or we will not do it. We will be solution seekers and problem solvers. For me, there is no middle ground.

Stephenson's view of faculty is also supported by Lakewood, Washington–based Clover Park Technical College Special Assistant to the President Mabel Edmonds: "Faculty plays a critical role in that they educate/train/develop the workforce. They should stay current with trends, occupational demands, business/industry needs, and skill gaps. They should also engage with employers so they maintain relevant curriculum, technologies, and advisory committees."

Chapter Ten

The Role of Community College Workforce Development Leaders and Staff in Workforce Development

Most community colleges have an organizational unit devoted to workforce development. We asked the Thought Leaders what role that unit's leaders and staff should play in workforce development.

Sumiton, Alabama–based Bevill State Community College President Larry A. Ferguson emphasized the importance of properly training workforce development staff for their role:

> We went through a process several years ago where we redesigned all of the workforce development units of our 16 colleges. They were rebranded and were called Workforce Solutions. We also reexamined what those individuals should do.
>
> One thing you have to be careful of is that often staff members will be given titles relating to workforce development but they haven't had adequate training to prepare them for that. To my knowledge, there is no major in that anywhere. Make sure they are adequately trained and that they are clear about what they should do and what results they should achieve.
>
> Mission creep is a problem. That happens when we throw things at workforce development units because we do not know where else to assign them. Be very careful that the activities they are being assigned truly are linked to community, economic, and workforce development. I think it is a clarification of roles—an understanding of what is needed and not letting that department within the college just become a catchall.
>
> I know you have probably seen that happen or heard talk of that. We must be concrete and precise. Front-line workforce development staff meets with clients, performs needs analysis, contracts for the training, and shepherds pro-

jects through to completion. We should give them short targeted goals—three to five—to guide their performance each year. It is not magic, but I think it is all about clarity of goals.

Kenosha, Wisconsin–based Gateway Technical College Vice President of Business and Workforce Solutions Deborah Davidson explains how important it is for workforce development staff members to base what they do on genuine employer needs:

> My division serves as a research and development arm of the college. It can take academic divisions longer to create a new program. Oftentimes, companies are coming in and saying "We need it now." We have the flexibility to put training together rather quickly. It may be credit; it may be noncredit. In many colleges the academic division only offers credit-bearing courses and a contract training division only offers noncredit. At Gateway, both divisions may offer credit or noncredit courses, which allows for better collaboration.
>
> We develop short-term training for a company and then seek to understand if the need is something many companies need. If that is the case, we may transition the program to the academic division and suggest turning that into a longer-term program.

Lakewood, Washington–based Clover Park Technical College Special Assistant to the President Mabel Edmonds emphasizes the importance of workforce development staff members in reaching out to, and meeting the needs of, local employers:

> Workforce development leaders and staff are those closest to the workforce system and how it operates. Their primary role is to ensure the President/faculty/staff at their college stay abreast of workforce trends, needs, issues, funding sources, and best practices.
>
> Another role is to facilitate the planning, implementation, and assessment of the college's workforce development delivery system and outcomes. For the most part, workforce development leaders and staff are knowledgeable and do a good job. However, improvement is needed in providing the leadership necessary to have an effective workforce development system within colleges. Silos still exist; it's difficult to bring faculty and staff together to take stock, coordinate, and collaborate at a high level to achieve the desired outcomes.

Chapter Eleven

What Community Leaders Can Do to Support Community Colleges

Community colleges are the nexus between education, communities, and community organizations. It is not just the role of community colleges to support the community; they must also be supported by community leaders. For that reason, we asked the Thought Leaders what community leaders can do to support community colleges.

In answering that question, Charlotte, North Carolina–based Central Piedmont Community College President P. Anthony Zeiss notes that

> first they need to be advocates for the college. They need to be advocates with policy makers and anyone else that they talk to.
>
> When I first came to Charlotte, I had an experience with our economic development department at the Chamber of Commerce. The first day I got on this job, on December 1, 1972, I met a woman on the airplane. She was a site selector, and she told me she would go to Greensboro and Spartanburg but was flying into Charlotte. I asked, Why aren't you looking into Charlotte, because it is a better place to go. That statement astonished her. I gave her information and called the Chamber of Commerce. The Chamber attracted her company to Charlotte. I thought that experience would signal to economic developers I want to be a player with them.
>
> It took about six years before I could convince them that one key incentive for relocating or new start-up plants is the ability to get and keep skilled workers. Since then, they have had us at the table. But it took a long time to convince the economic development people because they wanted to boast about the local university. And I finally had to come out and say, "Most of the jobs you are recruiting are not university graduate jobs."
>
> The county supports our collaborative with 15 community colleges in a 29-county region in North and South Carolina and appreciates our collabora-

tions with the public university. Students who want to transfer to the university go on as juniors.

Sumiton, Alabama–based Bevill State Community College President Larry A. Ferguson notes:

> I think it is a two-way street. I think they can reach out, not just to the President, but to deans and to staff involved with workforce development. They can offer help and support and work to create a feedback loop where we are working together to solve collective problems.
>
> Businesses rarely feel that contacting the President is necessarily their role. So I don't think they take those opportunities. Even they will have to think more entrepreneurially and risk contacting the college. Most colleges, even if they are not as far along as some of ours are, understand the importance of that and will respond if contacted.

Warren, Michigan–based Macomb Community College President James Jacobs stresses the importance of flexibility in community–college relations:

> We have two kinds of relationships. The first relationship is with the large businesses. The large businesses must see our institutions as the starting point for many of their students. I want to use an example, and this is a real one. You go to a company like Microsoft. Microsoft will tell you they don't hire community college students. They will tell you they only hire people with four-year degrees, and they only hire from 20 engineering schools around the country they have relationships with.
>
> But if you ask Microsoft this question—How many people you have hired from these four-year schools started at a community college?—then they get interested. For the large companies, the relationship with the community college is one in which we are indirect, but we are crucial because the skills we teach will make a student successful at the four-year school. We give them the practical experience to go into a job with the knowledge of what to do.
>
> You can hire an engineering student from the University of Michigan who has never been inside a factory, never seen a metal cut, and never designed a part. But if employers hire the students who may go to the University of Michigan, they will go into the classes at the University of Michigan knowing how to operate a machine and knowing what kinds of things can be designed that can be made. The start-up time for community college students is far less. That is why our nursing students often do better on the nursing test than the four-year nursing students, because we give them practical experience. That's the sales pitch to the large companies.
>
> To the smaller companies, we are the direct trainer and educator. Small employers may want their students to go on to school. But they will hire directly out of our programs. We have to maintain ties with them in a different way. Understanding how to do that and the complexities of that are the future for dealing with business.
>
> One final point. Obviously there are many policy issues we don't have time to get into. But policy issues around Pell grants, policy issues around the

Perkins Act, and policy issues around the Workforce Investment Act—all those things which we are affected by need also to have allies in the business community supporting us. If General Motors and Ford and Chrysler want to weigh in on Pell grants so our noncredit students who become apprentices can use Pell grants in a way to develop their skills, that will help us a great deal in the U.S. Department of Education. Now, to the degree we can do all those things, that is another issue. That is where colleges working with large companies can move policy levers to influence the future needs of the workforce.

Prestonsburg, Kentucky–based Big Sandy Community and Technical College President Devin Stephenson explains that community leaders must take steps to understand the college:

> Community leaders must realize our value in community, economic, and workforce development and how integrally those three aspects of our mission are woven. I believe, as a college president, it is my charge to ensure community leaders understand we are the heartbeat of the community. I envision our institution as the premier economic, workforce, and community development engine of this region. However, community colleges are often overlooked in this role.
>
> If you review the statistics for community colleges, 93 percent of our graduates either stay in the community or will return upon completion of their four-year degree. We are making a $172 million annual economic impact on this region.
>
> I just don't think some communities realize how vital we are, and I think it is incumbent on me as the community college President to help them see it clearly and help them see it now. So, when I speak at Rotary Clubs, Kiwanis Clubs, Chamber meetings, I speak about our impact and attempt to get the audience to imagine the community without the community college. I always ask the question, "What would this region be without the community college?"
>
> Understanding our college and what we do in fulfilling our mission will lead to stronger support. We must foster community understanding of who we are and what we do. It is a never-ending journey of educating the public as to who we are, what we do, and the impact we make. Once there is a clear understanding, then opportunities and possibilities can and will happen. It is at that point the college will become involved and active in the life of community development.

President Charles Terrell of Eastern West Virginia Community and Technical College in Moorefield, West Virginia, sees the role of community leaders as being rooted in talking up education—and the college:

> We are doing our job facilitating. We are helping with taking the initiative in community development, and community leaders can be the best people for marketing. If community leaders talk about the college in a positive way, that is the best marketing in the world. It occurs by word of mouth. Community leaders can be our true advocates.

I am very passionate about what we do, and I say "we." I get excited when I go out into the community. At every presentation in the community, I always start off by saying what is happening at your community college. When business and industry partners donate equipment or someone to teach a seminar, we refer to them as *shareholders* rather than as *stakeholders*. They have made an investment in their community college, and so it becomes important for us to show them that return on investment with quality graduates or students that come from workforce training. It all goes to that relationship. We want to print shareholder certificates telling them they own a part of this institution—they are a part of this college—it's their community college.

Kenosha, Wisconsin–based Gateway Technical College Vice President of Business and Workforce Solutions Deborah Davidson thinks that

community leaders must first visit the college. People have impressions that may be dated. Gateway is over 100 years old, and people think they know us because they attended the college 15, 25, or 50 years ago!

In order to engage our community, we open all our facilities to community groups to use at no charge. We want them on campus, as we have done much to change the image by remodeling the campuses over the last five to six years. As we remodel, we add interior windows looking into the classroom because we want visitors and guests to see each classroom and lab. At our manufacturing center visitors will see 3-D printers, CNC mills and lathes, robots, automated systems, and electronics. Visitors form positive impressions from that. We call this the Gateway Experience and it includes the look and feel of the environment at each campus.

Image is about building community awareness so community leaders think of Gateway first. Gateway collaborates with our sister technical colleges (there are 16 colleges throughout the state that are part of the Wisconsin Technical College System) to identify expertise beyond our own capabilities. In doing this we are able to fill most needs identified by businesses and organizations in our community. As a taxpayer-funded organization, we want community leaders to see us as *their* community resource for training.

Clover Park Technical College Special Assistant to the President Mabel Edmonds of Lakewood, Washington, succinctly explains what community leaders should do: "Community leaders can better support colleges by utilizing the expertise the colleges have, identifying resource development opportunities/funding, and recognizing good work."

Chapter Twelve

Trends Affecting the Ability of Community Colleges to Meet Needs of Future Students

Everyone knows that the world is changing—and it is changing fast. That fact affects community colleges as much as it affects businesses, government agencies, and nonprofit entities. We asked Thought Leaders what trends affect the ability of community colleges to meet needs of future students.

According to Gateway Technical College President and Chief Executive Bryan Albrecht of Kenosha, Wisconsin, "I would like to see more community colleges invested in public–private partnerships. The public–private partnership draws in that local ownership. Another trend is customizing curriculum and the educational experience. The alignment between two- and four-year colleges can make it easier for adults to attend and complete college."

According to Harrisburg Area Community College President John J. Sygielski of Harrisburg, Pennsylvania:

> At HACC, our board of trustees and employees are engaged in discussions about the trends impacting our enrollment activities and operations and how to remain relevant and valuable to the communities we serve. Personally, I think some of the many trends I could mention are exciting, for they are forcing us to rethink our educational business models.
>
> A few of the many trends I will address are those we in higher education are facing together. Resources—or the lack of them—are impacting us most significantly. Reductions from federal, state, and local agencies have made us review our operations and reach out to our philanthropic communities in new and creative ways. The changes in technology are trends that are forcing us to

engage and deliver training and education in new and exciting ways. I, especially, cannot wait to see what the use of artificial intelligence will mean for the way we engage learners in acquiring and using information.

The changing demographics also present us—as facilitators of learning—with opportunities to address a nontraditional-age and more diverse population throughout our 10-county service region. Many of these individuals will be un- or underemployed, in need of skills upgrading and/or a second or third career. Finally, I believe a more intense discussion about governance and accountability will continue to intensify at the federal and state levels.

President P. Anthony Zeiss of Central Piedmont Community College, based in Charlotte, North Carolina, notes that

there will be three challenges facing community colleges in the future. The first challenge is to get over the notion that tradition is the only way to do things and to be open to new concepts, new ideas, and new ways to do things. That's scary. Many leaders at the community college level do not want to do that because they fear alienating their faculty. If we gain the trust of our faculty, they get involved in innovation. But if we surprise them, we have not built trusting relationships and our efforts will not go far.

The second challenge is funding. Public funding for community colleges is dropping like a stone. Seventy-one percent of the federal budget is taken by entitlements. That leaves education competing for dwindling funds available in federal and state government coffers. About three-quarters of the states' budgets once funded education, and now Medicaid and other federal mandates are taking money away, so education funding is cut at the federal and state levels. Community colleges must learn how to be more entrepreneurial, how to collaborate better, and how to raise money on their own. Otherwise, they may cease to be prominent in their communities.

The third challenge involves regulations. We are bombarded with regulations, and we can hardly keep up with them. Central Piedmont Community College had to hire a full-time person to take care of new Title IX regulations because the federal Department of Education reexamined Title IX. The regulations have been expanded beyond sports and now deal with sexual misconduct, according to their interpretation. We must teach all students, faculty, staff, and administrators about sexual misconduct. We have to hire someone to handle all grievances, complaints, or innuendoes about sexual misconduct. We are being regulated to death and diverted from what the real mission of the college is because people get these social and political agendas, and they place them on us, and we have to become compliant. That costs much money, time, and effort.

Let me give you another example. Two colleges are under indictment because they are offering online classes that the federal government, under the ADA [Americans with Disabilities Act], is saying, "People who can't read what's on that computer who are visually impaired or people who are hearing impaired and can't hear what is being said in those online classes are not being accommodated." Where is that going to go? That could be the end of online classes if they keep pushing it, because redesigning every course to accommodate every possible disability will make it impossible to afford anything. It's very frustrating!

I can fight them and raise the money to comply, but the cost is huge. Complying would take up most of my time. I can be innovative and convince my faculty to be innovative, and that's very rewarding. But dealing with all these regulations is paralyzing us. The problem is that the federal government used to pass laws. But now federal or state department executives go around Congress or state legislatures, reinterpreting rules or making new rules, however they want.

I wrote a book about the future labor shortage coming and the skills gap in 2005 called *Get 'em while They're Hot.* I devoted much time in that book to telling corporate leaders and HR people that if they want to compete in the talent war and win it, they better focus on becoming a great place to work. The organization must establish a reputation for fair pay, careers, and promotions. If you don't have that, you will be pirated and you should be pirated. Talented workers will go other places. You can't just say it's a good place to work; you must make it a good place to work.

We have partnerships, for instance. We needed to bring more manufacturing into this area for the Global Vision. We look around and ask, Where can we find more manufacturing jobs? And we ask:

"Who produces the best manufacturing jobs?"

Hmm?

"Germany."

Yes, Germany produces the best manufacturing in the world.

Germany has a negative growth population. Consequently, many of their companies are moved offshore to find workers. We want them to come here. Consequently, we are trying to become the most German-friendly college in America. The upshot of that is we now have a partnership with a German government chamber of commerce and industry. As far as we know, we are the only college allowed to teach and confer German manufacturing certifications to our students. These are certifications that German company owners value highly, and they couldn't get them just anywhere. That gives us a great advantage when we recruit German companies here to say we are here. It's a win-win for everybody.

We have another partnership with Festo, a large automation equipment company. Festo wants to get into the American market, and more American companies want Festo equipment because it is viewed as the best. We have a big laboratory, and they've helped us with that. We plan to train people on any equipment they sell. We have many initiatives going on like that.

Sumiton, Alabama–based Bevill State Community College President Larry A. Ferguson sees several other trends affecting community colleges:

Funding is one challenge. The other, though, is can we meet the demands just based off our population numbers? We have heard for years about the baby boomers retiring. In many states and many communities, the student population exiting our secondary schools is flat or is decreasing. How are we going to meet those demands in the workforce? I think we can.

I believe we know we also need to address some of our immigration issues. We need to engage a different population, a different diverse population, and provide them with the educational services and tools they need to succeed in the workforce.

The last point I would make about the future is the continuing conversation we have with Lumina and the Gates Foundation about industry certifications. Is there more value to an industry certification than a credential offered at the community college, or should the community college credential prepare students to get that appropriate industry certification? I know, for us, we have linked almost all of our programs to industry-based certifications, but those will become more important. There will have to be focus, even at the federal level, on how we sort those out.

In Kansas, they have identified a list of those credentials, and they are paying for those for students to attain them. They have identified a list, and I think we will see a move toward that on industry certifications. If you are going into manufacturing, you need this MSCC certification, or whatever it might be. Industry certifications will play a part in what we are doing.

Prestonsburg, Kentucky–based Big Sandy Community and Technical College President Devin Stephenson also points to funding issues as a trend:

I think the decline of state financial resources will continue to impede our ability to serve. We have seen double-digit declines in state support over the past decade and it appears to be a continuing trend. Also, I believe we are on a long journey of turning the tide of public opinion toward community colleges and our importance in revitalizing this nation's economy. We have made great strides. We are seeing a shift in degree demands and there is a major tilt in the labor market composition that favors individuals who possess credentials and skills away from the traditional four-year degree.

I also believe high school administrators need to become more knowledgeable of the demands of the new workforce. It is my experience that because of all the demands on today's high school counselors, they do not have the time and adequate resources to guide students for career success. In fact, more students come to our community college in the "decision zone" rather than having a good understanding and proper preparation for the careers that fit and will lead to a job with a sustainable family wage. We all have to do a better job creating seamless career pathways and educating our youth very early regarding opportunities and fit. We must do a better job with career development and with building career expectations.

One major problem is that we have not raised the expectations of high school students about what their future can and should look like. They see a new car, a new house, and that picture is pretty and they believe they can get there, but we are failing these students by not providing realistic expectations regarding the pathway necessary to achieve that dream.

In the future colleges will employ fewer full-time people, and I think that because of technology. I think online education will reach 50 percent or more of our credit-hour production. Much of our teaching and training will be done virtually in a college-without-walls setting.

I think you will see less expansion in physical facilities. Now, I am not saying I am a prophet in a nonprofit organization, but if the trends continue as we have seen them in the past few years, higher education will not look the same in 10 years. Delivery will be responsive, accountability will be higher than ever before, and measurement of success will be based upon performance and success. It is challenging to think about, but exciting if you are willing to change.

President Charles Terrell of Moorefield-based Eastern West Virginia Community and Technical College points to trends in unfunded mandates and public–private partnerships. As he says:

Dealing with unfunded mandates is a trend. There are many unfunded mandates. That links to the compliance issue. We must have more personnel devoted to it, and we are not getting any funding to bring in that additional support.

We also see another trend with public–private partnerships. As we see diminishing public funds, we ask, How can colleges get more involved in public–private partnerships? That is how we are growing our business incubator. We call it a "new-biz launchpad." We don't own the building. We rent the building from an entrepreneur, and we have contracted with an individual to be an Entrepreneur in Residence. They are not faculty members; they are not staff members. They are contracted to provide this service, and we pay rent for using their building. We are trying to get creative.

Eastern is unique because we have contracted to have an Information Technology Director. That person is associated with the West Virginia Network. That person is affiliated with that network where there is a wealth of information and other subject experts that work on the network to which this director now has access. If we hired somebody on campus, that person would have that same network.

The private–public relationships in the building are already taking place as we need new facilities. I have already shared the vision we would like to see in our business, IT, and co-working space. I mentioned at an ARC strategic planning meeting that one of our future expansions would include spaces for private organizations. We are allowing individuals to rent space from us to have a small business on campus.

The issue is broadband access. We've got fiber here at the college. Why wouldn't we use a future college facility to provide small businesses access to fiber and have that private–public partnership here? I think that will be the trend. I think it will continue. We have to blend and merge resources.

Another trend, and this is positive, is that community colleges have a bright future because they are involved in the community. The reason we had Noah Brown with the professional development program with our board of governors was to give them updates on President Obama's America's College Promise. Will that be a trend? Will that be the outcome, that community colleges will promote greater access and be almost like public education? It is not a new idea. It was proposed in the Truman Commission Report in the 1950s.

By expanding relationships with business and industry, they may provide scholarships or they may pay for training programs. I think that is a positive trend for us.

We have nine two-year institutions that circle Eastern. I would like to put together, before the end of the year, a summit of all institutions and discuss our problems. We sit down at the table and we form these relations. How do we form, maybe, our consortium for when we apply for any potential grants with the federal government? That would have a huge impact because it would cover three states—Maryland, Virginia, and West Virginia. I think it is a trend to form these large collaborative consortiums.

Kenosha, Wisconsin–based Gateway Technical College Vice President of Business and Workforce Solutions Deborah Davidson sees increasingly flexibility as a trend. As she notes:

A number of years ago when there was an increase in dislocated workers, Gateway looked at our traditional academic calendar and determined that we were not adequately poised to offer the flexibility expected by these students. We moved to a three-semester, year-round calendar. Each semester is 15 weeks in length and allows for continuous enrollment opportunities for our students. Each program determines, through their advisory committees, whether they will offer their program year-round. If they do not offer it year-round, the students can take their general education courses in the summer semester and their occupational program courses in fall and spring semesters.

In order to implement this, faculty work two of the three semesters and are off for one semester. This provides greater flexibility for the faculty. The average age of our students is 32, so we know that we are better serving their needs by providing continuous enrollment opportunities that allow for quicker completion.

The college has instituted a new scheduling system that looks at program course requirements, student scheduling preferences, and room utilization in order to schedule courses at the optimal time. This will likely lead to more evening, more weekend, and more online offerings.

Another trend is that there are more people stopping in and out of education. Career pathways, credentialing, and prior learning assessment have become critical in higher education and I believe we are doing many things to address this. We have a Career Pathways Manager at the college who is working with faculty and industry advisory committees to develop pathway maps for each of our 60 programs. The pathway includes certificates, diplomas, degrees, apprenticeships, industry certifications, and the use of prior learning assessment to allow students to move more seamlessly between career and education pathways.

Using networks is not a new trend for community colleges, but it has become increasingly important for each of us to learn from each other. The timeline for developing new programs, processes, and institute new ways of serving our customers (students and employers) has been shortened. Reaching out to colleagues across the state and nation can considerably reduce the development timeline. We don't benchmark ourselves only against our state colleagues, we look at best practices across the country and then determine how to make it work locally. We participate in the National Coalition of Advanced Technology Centers, the National Coalition of Certification Centers, the American Association of Community Colleges, and the International Technology and Engineering Educators Association, to name a few.

Gateway is a model college and we are always looking at ways to improve. One of the two goals in our strategic plan is to "Create a Culture of Excellence." One way in which we addressed this was the implementation of Lean Six Sigma. All employees have a white belt, 25 employees earned green belts, and five employees earned black belts.

A white-belt certification means understanding the terminology of lean and the terminology of Six Sigma. A green belt indicates that the individual participated in a project that addressed an identified improvement need in the college. A black belt is earned by an individual who has led project teams for more impactful projects leading to greater hard and soft cost savings. Because of our role in lean, we collaborated with a vendor and created a Center of Excellence in Lean for Education, and we work with other schools to mentor them through the process and implementation of lean at their institution.

Lakewood, Washington–based Clover Park Technical College Special Assistant to the President Mabel Edmonds points to several trends affecting community colleges:

Trends that might affect the ability of colleges to meet the needs of future students include the following: (1) decline in funding from the federal/state/local sources; (2) rising cost of maintaining and building the infrastructure needed, such as technology and training equipment; and (3) high cost of tuition/books/fees, which will make it more difficult for the target populations to afford college.

In 10 years, I envision colleges in vibrant and wealthier communities having state-of-the-art campuses, technologies that would be difficult to imagine today; those in less affluent communities will be unable to serve their residents adequately and meet the needs of businesses/industries to grow their economy.

Chapter Thirteen

Conversations with Business Leaders about the Role of Community Colleges

We asked Thought Leaders this question: "Imagine that you were having a conversation with business leaders from your community about the role of community colleges. What would you tell them about that role?" This chapter describes how the Thought Leaders answered that important question. Not all Thought Leaders addressed this question.

According to Special Assistant to the President Mabel Edmonds of Clover Park Technical College in Lakewood, Washington, "Our role is to help employers develop the workforce they need for the employment opportunities they have today and the ones they will have in the future. We want to assist employers to be competitive in a global economy."

According to Blytheville–based Arkansas Northeastern College President James Shemwell:

> People today, especially younger people, read less. Their attention span is shorter, and so we have to facilitate. Rather than lamenting that, we just have to deal with it and facilitate learning through active participation and through real-life examples.
>
> We have to get over lamenting what's wrong and recognize that students are coming to college less self-sufficient and less accountable. We will have to do what we can to slowly ingrain self-sufficiency and accountability. That is just how it is. We have to deal with situations as they are and not as we wish they were. We are creating the future, and we have to get over complaining about present conditions and solve the problems.
>
> We need to be looking at fewer textbooks and use more open resources. I think you will see more things online. I think you will see more hybrid classes.

I think you will see more flexible scheduling and more emphasis on social amenities.

Chapter Fourteen

Other Thoughts

In the course of our interviews, our Thought Leaders raised additional issues that went beyond answers to our predetermined interview questions. These ideas are worth repeating. The Thought Leaders made comments on such topics as:

- *Planning for succession in community colleges*
- *Finding qualified instructors*
- *Keeping teaching talent updated*
- *Recruiting to community colleges from high schools*
- *Adjusting to recessions and economic conditions*
- *Building a team through support coalitions*
- *Negotiating effective working relationships among boards of directors*
- *Resolving conflicts*
- *Partnering with school districts*
- *Using assessments in workforce development*
- *Building and sharing a common vision of workforce development for a community/region*
- *Working with employers as critically important for community colleges*
- *Preparing students for the world of work*

This chapter examines these issues in the order they are listed above.

PLANNING FOR SUCCESSION IN COMMUNITY COLLEGES

Several community college leaders pointed to the importance of succession planning in community colleges.

As Harrisburg, Pennsylvania–based Harrisburg Area Community College President John J. Sygielski points out:

> With senior faculty and administrators retiring at alarming rates, I and the college's board of trustees have intentionally tasked our Office of Human Resources professional development department to create and implement a leadership development program that identifies and supports emerging leaders within the college.
>
> In fact, I have challenged my administrative team with identifying and recommending a diverse pool of emerging leaders within their units so we can begin a process to review and recommend those individuals into the leadership development program. We want to make certain it is a diverse pool of individuals so the individuals promoted will look more like the changing demographics of the communities we serve.
>
> This all means by thinking differently we will inform our past and current culture with new ways of engaging all of our constituent groups that are relevant and impactful. Finally, we are beginning to cross-train individuals within specific departments to ensure continuity in operations in case a senior leader wins the lottery and departs the institution unexpectedly.

Palatine, Illinois–based William Rainey Harper College President Ken Ender agrees. As he sees it, "It's important for community college presidents to develop their direct reports. Deans, for instance, are individuals of particular interest at our community college. They will most likely become community college presidents. The President should give them experience and exposure to his or her work as part of planning and developing a workable succession plan."

Cleveland, Ohio–based Cuyahoga Community College Executive Vice President of Workforce, Community, and Economic Development William Gary also points to the importance of succession planning:

> Succession planning should be policy in all organizations to sustain growth and organizational continuity and culture. A key component of my restructuring of Tri-C's Workforce Division was the creation of a succession strategy and plan. This is a major priority of the college and one necessary to ensure a high-performing quality organization: Who will take your place? What qualifications must they possess? What training is required? What skills gaps exist and how will these be filled? What organization acceptance is required for the plan? If something were to happen to me today, who could the President call upon, internally, to assume my position? And would he endorse that recommendation? That's the key—would the President endorse that and support it?
>
> I'm not sure, quite frankly, if the President has initiated or implemented a succession strategy. But let's keep in mind, he's now beginning his third year, and I am sure that once he builds or completes the building of his team that includes me, I hope, he will then say, "This is the plan for succession that will include internal upgrading"—I have not seen that yet, but it's definitely within

his purview because he's definitely that kind of person and that kind of strategist.

FINDING QUALIFIED INSTRUCTORS

Several Thought Leaders explained that a continuing challenge they face is to find qualified instructors.

In the words of Kenosha, Wisconsin–based Gateway Technical College President and Chief Executive Bryan Albrecht:

> It can be difficult to recruit professionals in skilled occupations. We work with our companies to address the skill gap. Experienced technical employees are retiring, leaving a void in the knowledge and skills to maintain competitiveness. We put together programs that allow those retirees to teach. That gives them a flexible resource. The retiree gets a little income. And it adds value to the community.
>
> As a community college, we still get to take advantage of their skills. We are doing much with retirees, bringing them back to be adjunct instructors for us. We also put together a unique model: it is a three-semester-a-year calendar approach so our instructors have flexibility to teach two or three semesters. That gives instructors more flexibility in teaching schedules and makes our community college more attractive to future teachers.
>
> But finding qualified instructors remains a challenge. Just like in industry, we must find top-notch talent and make sure that we have the resources to support them. That allows us to put together positive lab experiences for students so they succeed in the classroom. We make sure that the teachers get the support they need in the classroom.

That is a view with which Tempe, Arizona–based Rio Salado College President Chris Bustamante agrees:

> We have been identifying qualified instructors for more than 30 years and have a host of trainers and teachers. In our educational service partnerships, our trainers are the same ones that companies already use, and we certify them so that we can offer these courses. In our credit-for-training programs we credential instructors under an occupational standard that complies with guidelines set by the district and our accreditors. We certify instructors from the company who meet these standards in part because they have been trainers in their respective fields for many years. Because we are doing this with our business partners and using their instructors, it is much easier to identify qualified instructors and offer the programs.
>
> In our dual enrollment program, a program that provides opportunity for high school students to earn high school and college credit simultaneously during the regular school day, we certify on-site high school instructors to teach community college–level courses. They must meet the same credential requirements that our residential faculty must meet.

The advantage of partnering with companies and high schools is that we use their infrastructure, resources, and equipment for the educational programs offered at their facilities. This partnership model is very efficient, cost-effective, and sustainable.

A similar view was expressed by Bevill State Community College President Larry A. Ferguson of Sumiton, Alabama:

I will be honest. The best way to find them is to identify people who recently retired from an industry sector and are still highly skilled. We have had much success with that. We need someone not out of that industry sector for long and who still has up-to-date skills.

We work with engineers from different sectors who do part-time work with us to facilitate this training. We are also heavily invested in getting our full-time faculty the professional development they need. They participate in externships. In the summertime, if they have time, they may work in industry for a month (30 days). That is critical to keeping their skills at the cutting edge at a world-class level so we can deliver first-rate training.

KEEPING TEACHING TALENT UPDATED

Finding qualified instructors may be a challenge. But so is keeping those instructors equipped with current skills. As Kenosha, Wisconsin–based Gateway Technical College President and Chief Executive Bryan Albrecht explains:

We have a professional development program we require all faculty to be a part of. New teachers have a mentoring program. We also have a link for new teachers so they can go back into the field during the off-semester and participate in an externship so they work in industry. And they get reimbursed and paid for their participation.

We have extensive professional development funding so faculty can earn additional credentials and attend professional development conferences. But what's driving that activity is our advisory committee, and their expectations that our programs are aligned with industry certification and industry standards. We ask instructors to have both academic and industry credentials in related fields. In welding it might be AWS certification and automotive NATEF certification or in health care it might be a nursing license. There's an expectation that instructors remain current in whatever it is they teach.

RECRUITING TO COMMUNITY COLLEGES FROM HIGH SCHOOLS

Instructors are important, but a pipeline of students is also important. According to Kenosha, Wisconsin–based Gateway Technical College President and Chief Executive Bryan Albrecht:

> We have several partnerships through our high schools. We co-run a high school called the Lakeview Academy in which the junior and senior courses are taught by Gateway Technical College faculty for college credit. We have academy models in place, and articulation with our area schools.
>
> This year Gateway served over 4,000 high school students. We reach into our high schools and even into middle schools. We run camps during the summer months for science, technology, engineering, and mathematics [STEM] education. We contact our elementary schools and run community programs for elementary school teachers. We really try to open our campus as much as we can for all educational levels. It builds community awareness of our college, and it creates an awareness of all the programs available to help young people make positive career choices by experiencing it for themselves.

ADJUSTING TO RECESSIONS AND ECONOMIC CONDITIONS

Community colleges must adjust their operations to economic conditions. After all, economic conditions do affect enrollments and employment prospects. As Kenosha, Wisconsin–based Gateway Technical College President and Chief Executive Bryan Albrecht points out:

> Economic conditions is one challenge we face in the world of community colleges. Gateway saw a 35 percent increase in enrollment from 2009 to 2012, and then the economy got a little better. When the economy is strong, enrollments level out. Employment is high for us right now in our respective county community. Over 5,000 new jobs have been added locally over the last year. That means people are working, which is good.
>
> But that also means they don't have time to go back to school, or they are not choosing to go back for higher education. When enrollment slows down, it limits college growth. The college doesn't have as many new programs. We can't be quite as aggressive in customizing what we already do because no revenue stream supports it.
>
> But we are looking at ways to solve that problem, such as offering more hybrid programs. We also integrate online and on-site programs. We went to a year-around calendar. We have three semesters per year so students can go to school all year long at Gateway and not have to take time off over the summer months. We are working diligently on customizing our training so our specialized programs can be on the employers' sites. These efforts have helped to keep strong enrollments at our college.

BUILDING A TEAM THROUGH SUPPORT COALITIONS

As Kenosha, Wisconsin–based Gateway Technical College President and Chief Executive Bryan Albrecht explains, "I'm fortunate to have been appointed to roles on different committee boards. But most of the time, I either reappoint a dean or take a dean with me. Our Deans are very active because they know in their own way where I would go with a decision. I don't decide for them, but they know to ask, 'Here's the expectations Dr. Albrecht would have; now how can I rally our team to make that happen?'"

NEGOTIATING EFFECTIVE WORKING RELATIONSHIPS AMONG BOARDS OF DIRECTORS

According to Kenosha, Wisconsin–based Gateway Technical College President and Chief Executive Bryan Albrecht:

> We have an onboarding process for all employees on the Gateway journey. Every employee goes through a 12- to 18-month onboarding process. I meet with every employee the week he or she starts the job. We talk about history, culture, and what it's like to move to a different community. I tell them my background, and it's more of an open exchange of backgrounds.
>
> We describe the governing structure of our college, the reporting mechanisms, and how to get ideas across. Then I have a weekly message I send to each employee, which is an open door, basically, to keep us communicating. It's usually something that's kind of clever and fun. This Monday, I had written about one of our STEM camps and I quoted one third-grader because he said something that was funny. That's an invitation for any employee to send me a quick response.
>
> One employee may write in a note, "That's really funny, Dr. Albrecht, glad to know you are back, and here's what my young daughter did this summer." This form of open communication keeps the pulse of everything going, and I think it is key. We also do formal surveys called "Workplace Dynamics," where we survey all employees every year. We've been a top workplace winner for the last five years in a row for Southeast Wisconsin. We've built a culture around cooperation and communication. I think if we just stay active, transparent, and honest with our employees and everyone is trying to do a good job, I think we find that any employees' missteps result because they were not given clear direction on how to perform their jobs.

RESOLVING CONFLICTS

According to Kenosha, Wisconsin–based Gateway Technical College President and Chief Executive Bryan Albrecht, conflicts between workforce development professionals and economic development professionals are resolved in a consistent way. In his words:

We put them on the same team. This is where leadership steps in. If I know it, I immediately contact the County Executive or the Mayor, and we get together and discuss the dynamic of our teams, how we can help smooth that over, or create a separation of duties so everybody knows their responsibilities. We don't allow conflicts to fester or grow personal. We make the call. If we don't get along, then nobody wins. We figure out a way to either work cooperatively or separate duties.

Gateway hosts an economic development organization, and their staff are on campus. We also host the Small Business Development Center on campus and try to integrate the services with all our college services. The more we integrate them, the easier it is for people to align with the right service provider.

Executive Vice President of Workforce, Community, and Economic Development William Gary of Cleveland, Ohio–based Cuyahoga Community College states that he approaches "conflict resolution by, first, knowing when to ask forgiveness versus permission. Second, through collaboration and consensus building. Third, and foremost, remembering that our decisions should be aligned with and in the best interest of the student and our clients, and the mission of the college, not ourselves."

PARTNERING WITH SCHOOL DISTRICTS

According to Kenosha, Wisconsin–based Gateway Technical College Vice President of Business and Workforce Solutions Deborah Davidson:

Apprenticeship started at Gateway in Wisconsin 105 years ago. Our apprenticeship numbers have tripled over the last two years, and we have more companies that participate in apprenticeship for industrial, service, and construction trades. Wisconsin also has a strong Youth Apprenticeship Program, which can transition into an adult apprenticeship.

We work with all of our K–12 school districts across the tri-county area. Gateway has college connection staff in each high school at least one day per week to increase student awareness of the programs offered at the college. We recently announced the Gateway Promise, which helps ensure qualifying students seeking an education can begin their path to success through a Gateway Technical College degree. Through this program students may attend Gateway tuition-free and earn their associate degree.

USING ASSESSMENTS IN WORKFORCE DEVELOPMENT

Workforce development should not occur in a vacuum; rather, it should be based on careful assessments. According to Harrisburg, Pennsylvania–based Harrisburg Area Community College President John J. Sygielski:

Assessment is sort of like a Developing a Curriculum [DACUM] process. We work with the employer to understand what their employees do and what they must know to do it. We build an assessment tailored to those working in that job or at that company.

If potential employees demonstrate that they have skill gaps in our assessment, we provide the necessary training to close the gaps so workers can meet employer requirements. We analyze what employers need and then assess individuals so their skills match employer requirements. We also take this information and integrate it into our traditional credit programs, ensuring the courses/programs remain vibrant and relevant to what is needed in our 10-county service region.

BUILDING AND SHARING A COMMON VISION OF WORKFORCE DEVELOPMENT FOR A COMMUNITY/REGION

As a nexus for workforce development efforts in each community and region, community colleges should build and share a common vision of workforce development. In the words of Harrisburg, Pennsylvania–based Harrisburg Area Community College President John J. Sygielski:

We're getting better at working together, even though a river—which acts more like an ocean—separates the east from the west shore of the city of Harrisburg.

Since we are a region, we need to continually look at our workforce challenges regionally. Slowly, leaders within the region are being forced to create a vision because they are all competing for an educated workforce. In the five years I have been here, it is a conversation we are engaging in more through our collective workforce development meetings with municipalities and other profit and not-for-loss organizations.

As the City of Harrisburg is reorganizing itself financially, it is forcing us to put together a common vision for the region. Fortunately, over the past couple of years, businesses are relocating here, as seen in Cumberland County with the establishment of large distribution centers such as the creation of Amazon and UPS facilities in Carlisle, Pennsylvania, along I-81. In creating a unified vision for the region, it is imperative that we show successes so employers remain in the area and continue to relocate in our 10-county service region.

I believe an entity—like community colleges—should champion the workforce development vision at the state, regional, and/or local levels. However, in working with various private- and public-sector organizations, politics usually gets in the mix. When politics takes center stage, however, we sometimes see people with special interests pulling the strings. Having been here only five years, I have seen an increased understanding of the value of a community college, namely HACC, Central Pennsylvania's Community College, as an unbiased facilitator of championing a workforce vision.

It is our responsibility, I believe, to prepare individuals for the workplace, ensuring our curriculum aligns with the needs of local employers, and/or prepare our students to transfer into degree programs at four-year institutions throughout the Commonwealth of Pennsylvania and beyond. This fact presents exciting opportunities for us to educate people about why a community college, and not a four-year institution, could be the best fit for the workforce and economic development activities in the region, especially because many of the jobs of the future will not require a baccalaureate degree or higher.

In addition, our alumni pool is rich and 85 percent of our graduates stay within a 25-mile radius of any of our five campuses. Therefore, it is critical for community colleges, especially HACC, to promote the need for cooperation at all levels of education, business, and government, no matter what side of the river you are on!

WORKING WITH EMPLOYERS: CRITICALLY IMPORTANT FOR COMMUNITY COLLEGES

According to Sumiton, Alabama–based Bevill State Community College President Larry A. Ferguson:

> Employers typically focus on their bottom line. Their concern is about financial performance, and so they know they need a talented workforce. They know they need workers to do certain things, but often they can't even clearly articulate what they need.
>
> The example I gave earlier is probably one of the best. We worked closely with Toyota, going on their shop floor, doing observations by utilizing Work-Keys and other approaches along those lines—such as DACUM sessions—to isolate what it is, what competencies students must have to perform as advanced manufacturing technicians. Now that was not an easy process, and took us close to five years. But as a result of analyzing the data we became able to predict the success rate for students in the program. We need to foster that give-and-take relationship, even if it needs to be brutally honest. It has to be a collaborative relationship. We must work together.
>
> We do much customized training. We do not walk into a company and offer a menu list of programs. That is not what needs to happen. What needs to happen is a useful needs analysis of the workforce for that company to determine on what their workers must be trained. Training should not be driven by a shopping list. I think it's crucial that you get down to those hard conversations. All of our top colleges use a standardized needs-analysis form that drives us to ask company representatives the right questions so we can get to the root causes of their performance issues.

Palatine, Illinois–based William Rainey Harper College President Ken Ender believes that "there's a natural affinity between the community college and the local development board. We work hard to build and keep a working alliance and collaborative working relationships in this venue. We have a strong network of other community colleges in the region on workforce development goal issues. Ultimately it is the community college President's role to champion collaborations, alliances, and networks and give these career pathways a strong undergirding of general education components. The community college President should articulate that. The President must be the champion, broker, and thought leader of most interventions in his or her respective local and regional area."

PREPARING STUDENTS FOR THE COMMUNITY COLLEGE AND THE WORLD OF WORK

Students are, of course, critical to the success of community colleges. President James Jacobs, of Warren, Michigan–based Macomb Community College, explains that

> we have a close interaction with our high school partners, and we have something called Early College. We have about 650 high school students taking classes at the college, and we have career academies organized. We have a design career academy where students in high school can take courses in autobody design at the community college for free.
>
> We focus on juniors and seniors in high school. Although there may be sophomores, they are rare. We intend to increase the career academies. We also have an apprenticeship program where we have students going to high school and enrolled in apprenticeship programs. The goal of that program is for them to continue at the community college.
>
> The fundamental assumption is there are many things students can do in the workplace—and learning at the workplace is vital for students that go on.
>
> Let me jump to community development. It takes many forms. We can have issues of criminal justice; we can have issues of housing; we can have issues of senior citizens; we can have issues of child care. Now a college can play a role in many, somewhat; but it is primarily in collaboration with others. Serving as a collaborator, as a place where meetings can be held, as a sympathetic institution that can do events or workshops, is one function.
>
> But another function, which will increasingly become important—and this is again something that we are pioneering with a few other community colleges—is in precisely this area of community development. What's the unique aspect of a community college student? Ninety percent of community college students go back into the community they came from. If so, why not develop programs which teach community college students how to become community organizers so they can develop their community? Why is it necessary to bring in Ivy League students from national organizations to teach in junior high schools in communities where our students went to those junior high schools?
>
> We have started, with some other community colleges, what could be a fascinating pilot project. It is called the Community Learning Partnership (CLP), where we teach our students how to be active in their communities. That is more than service learning. Service is a piece, but this is more thinking about how we analyze the community, how we work to change it, and then develop it. Part of that is getting a job in a community-based organization and

going on to school, maybe in social work. Part of it is also organizing in the community because that is where they are from and that is where they will live.

If you look at a school like ours, which is a large institution, we have over 140,000 living alumni within 40 miles of our institution. Every family in our county has been touched by Macomb Community College. We can become an enormous force in community development. But we have to be careful. We can't overstep our mission or our reach. We have to work with those other organizations present in the community. We are not trying to replace what is there; rather, we are trying to enhance it. That is the first part.

Economic development here is where we get into something that's unfolding for community colleges. I can use my college as an example. Like many other communities, the community we are in went through a profound change during the Great Recession of 2008. Because of that, although the economy is doing better and the automobile industry is hiring, the jobs that exist in the industry will never replace what was lost.

The ability to have sustainable good jobs in the community becomes an important question for the community college. It isn't just that we react to what companies want in talent; rather, we also have to work on the demand side to encourage entrepreneurial activities. We have developed a center for entrepreneurial innovation and growth, which helps promote entrepreneurial activities among our students and does many things to have students pitch competitions and form companies.

We also have gotten our board of trustees and a large bank, JPMorgan Chase, to invest in an innovation fund run by the college. This innovation fund allows us to use grant monies to start up companies, provided they offer some form of employment opportunities to our students. We are seeding and creating jobs for our students, using the resources of the college. Two other colleges around the country are doing this. That will play a big role in community college activities.

Many events are unfolding. The days are over where you could just react to what employers wanted. Community colleges don't even respond well to what employers want to begin with. Often colleges do an excellent job once somebody comes to them. I think what we are talking about, however, is for the colleges to define what is unfolding and take actions to create jobs and develop talent that will be necessary for that future.

Kenosha, Wisconsin–based Gateway Technical College President and Chief Executive Bryan Albrecht notes that his college provides inducements for students to remain at home and work while participating in school. As he explains, "We have many youth apprenticeship programs where students work their senior year. They earn college credit and gain work experience that counts toward their apprenticeship. We have a program called Youth Options where students can take a college course at no cost to have them gain exposure to college-level course material. These program efforts help expose students to the value of education but also link back to workplace learning. We help connect work experience with college experience."

President P. Anthony Zeiss, of Charlotte, North Carolina–based Central Piedmont Community College, describes how his college prepares students for the world of work:

> We developed a technical training center on the Central Piedmont College campus. We worked with students who wanted to go self-paced—maybe because they were on shifts where they couldn't get traditional classes. They would come in and go at their pace in one of the 10 technological areas. They ranged from automotive to welding to whatever, you name it. It worked well.
>
> This program was open to everyone. We received a large grant from the U.S. Department of Labor to do this, and we put the curriculum together. Then we got a grant from HUD to build the Training Center Building. It was quite a process, and people were coming from all over the country to benchmark it. We couldn't get over the fact that it was hard to get faculty to understand that it's better to be a facilitator of learning rather than a dispenser of knowledge. However, not every teacher feels comfortable as a facilitator. That's the only explanation I have to account for why competency-based education stalled in the country after the early 1970s and 1980s. Thankfully, it is making a comeback today.

Part III

The International Perspective

Part III offers an international perspective, since the world's economy is increasingly a global, interlinked one. Community colleges exist in the United States. But in other countries, workforce development is managed in other ways. In Germany, apprenticeships are widely used. In China, the country is building its infrastructure of polytechnical institutions and vocational schools.

Chapter Fifteen

Interview with Weiping Shi

Professor and Director, Institute of Vocational and Adult Education, East China Normal University, and Vice President, China Society of Vocational and Technical Education

Interview conducted by email and returned on August 20, 2015. Edited by William J. Rothwell and reviewed and approved by Dr. Shi.

DEFINING WORKFORCE DEVELOPMENT

In a broad sense, workforce development educates adults to gain knowledge, competence, and attitude to be qualified for the professional post. In a narrow sense, workforce development is to train the workforce to increase job skills.

THE ROLE OF THE POLYTECHNIC IN WORKFORCE DEVELOPMENT

In China, higher vocational colleges play a significant role in workforce development. In 2013, there were 1,321 regular higher vocational colleges (HVC) in China. Higher vocational colleges have two important tasks. One is full-time diploma education; the other is further education, including adult short-cycle courses and training.

In 2013, there were 9,736,373 full-time students in HVC, with 3,183,999 new enrollments and 3,187,494 graduates, while 3,609,549 adult students were registered in part-time training courses. There were also 3,971,306 students engaged in short-cycle training courses in other formal programs in 2013. The full-time higher vocational colleges train the applied technical and skilled workforce through learning by doing. The higher vocational colleges are strengthening the further training for the working adults, although it is still weak compared with the U.S.A.

THE ROLE THE POLYTECHNIC PLAYS IN COMMUNITY DEVELOPMENT, ECONOMIC DEVELOPMENT, INDIVIDUAL CAREER COUNSELING, AND TRAINING

Polytechnic or higher vocational colleges should serve community development by using their intellectual capital, instruments, facilities, and other resources. They can open campuses, gyms, libraries, and labs to the community. They can also cooperate with local companies to develop new products, innovate with technology, and train workers to support local economic development.

In workforce development, individual career counseling should be given more attention. Higher vocational colleges should participate in improving the workers' competencies for their jobs, diagnosing individual weaknesses, developing the curriculum, and purposefully guiding or training workers.

BARRIERS OR CHALLENGES FACING POLYTECHNICS IN CARRYING OUT THEIR ROLES

Polytechnics or higher vocational colleges face the difficulties of fulfilling their roles in workforce development. Most teachers have no practical working experiences in companies and lack knowledge and competencies to carry out the purpose of diagnosing the weakness of workers in their job competencies, not to say purposefully developing the curriculum, guiding, or training workers for improving their working skills and competencies.

In the long term, the institution has no effective regulations or incentive mechanism to encourage the teachers to be committed to training. The government or external evaluation for the colleges has no valid indicators to drive college teachers to improve their training competencies.

HOW TECHNOLOGY IS CHANGING THE FACE OF EDUCATION

As we know, information technology has changed education to some extent. MOOCs have come to the higher vocational colleges. The information technology–based teaching and learning methods have been used widely in instruction. In 2013, there were 3,971,306 adult students engaged in short-cycle courses in web-based learning with higher institutions while 1,024,060 students graduated in the same year.

Technology will more widely be used in teaching and learning. But whatever technology changes, human beings, or teachers, remain the main force. Face-to-face teaching in the classroom is still the usual way of delivering education and training in China.

THE ROLE OF THE COLLEGE PRESIDENT IN WORKFORCE DEVELOPMENT

In China's system, the responsibility of the college President in workforce development is to have a strong connection and maintain the good relationship with the local industries and companies and to make sound policies to drive, encourage, and reward the teachers and other staff to work on local workforce development. It is equally important for the higher vocational college President to get local industries and companies deeply involved in the college administration and curriculum development.

Not every president will vigorously support their staff members to work on workforce development. The role of the President in job skills training for local workers hinges on their interests, thoughts, and ideas. It also depends on whether the College Party Secretary shares the same vision with the President, for in China the Party Secretary is usually sitting in the "driver's seat" in our system. The President and the Party Secretary, who pay more attention to job skills training or non-diploma short-cycle courses for workforce development, will be inclined to support training.

THE ROLE OF THE DEAN IN WORKFORCE DEVELOPMENT

It is the Dean's responsibility to ensure good planning for workforce development programs for certain local industry or companies using staff or facilities within the school or department, to mobilize all the resources available to support such activities, and to develop a good departmental culture that encourages involvement in local workforce development.

Deans with the vision that colleges should serve local companies and society in technology upgrading and high-tech applications would try their best to work on workforce development. If colleges have hard rules for this, the school or departments would have rigid indices to measure workforce development.

THE ROLE OF FACULTY MEMBERS IN
WORKFORCE DEVELOPMENT

The faculty members of polytechnics or higher vocational colleges play the role to implement workforce development programs. They should try to understand the employer's human resource demands, identify the weaknesses of the workforce in technology application and job skills, and develop the training programs accordingly. Teachers with the abilities to offer such training are ready for workforce development. Some do this due to personal interest. But rules and regulations should be there to drive more people to do the job.

THE ROLE OF POLYTECHNIC LEADERS AND STAFF IN
WORKFORCE DEVELOPMENT

Vice presidents for academics should incorporate workforce training into the college curriculum, help set up the research institution for workforce development, finance their research, and refine the policies to provide facilities for workforce development. Vice presidents for further education should incorporate workforce training into the social services of the college.

WHAT COMMUNITY LEADERS SHOULD DO BETTER TO
SUPPORT POLYTECHNICS

Community leaders should be involved in workforce training service when the workforce development team is formed. Their role is to offer in-time advice and help them improve their workforce development programs and services.

TRENDS AFFECTING POLYTECHNICS

In China, the importance of literacy and numeracy education is overlooked. Most curriculum reforms in higher vocational colleges are linked to job skills, which will affect the students for their sustainable development in their career. Hard (technical) skills are often favored over soft (interpersonal) skills in vocational education and training in Chinese vocational colleges, which have proven to be fatal mistakes in workforce development and even more harmful to postindustrial society. At a time of Internet+, or German Industry 4.0, or China Manufacturing 2015, technology will bring great change. That will change the curriculum in higher vocational colleges and also change the way of teaching and learning in workforce development.

Some problems will persist with higher vocational colleges that still have limited partnerships with industry. Some fail to attract master-workers or worker-masters with sufficient job skills and working expertise in industry. That leads to the irrelevance of training programs to the jobs, inexperienced skill training teachers, and limited involvement of industries in college vocational education implementation.

WHAT TO TELL BUSINESS LEADERS ABOUT THE ROLE OF POLYTECHNICS

Polytechnics:

- Help to build a better-quality workforce for local industries
- Help to promote better innovation in technology and industrial upgrading
- Help to form better learning organizations within companies and a learning society in community
- Help to have better development of working careers for every member of the community
- Help individuals have better skills, better careers, and better lives
- Help companies have workforces with better skills, build better products, deliver better service, and improve better economy

Chapter Sixteen

Interview with Hans-Peter Mengele

Chief Executive Officer, Karlsruhe Chamber of Commerce and Industry (IHK), Germany

Interview conducted by Dr. P. Anthony Zeiss and Vernon L. Carraway on September 3, 2015. Transcribed by Vernon L. Carraway; edited by William J. Rothwell and reviewed and approved by Dr. Mengele.

PLACE THE EMPHASIS ON COMPANY NEEDS

Content is imperative and has to be continuously modernized and adapted to industry needs. However, content is not the only thing. Look at any company. We have to look at what qualifications the company needs. That is a crucial starting point.

In the old world, you had universities, and they provided what their teachers thought were the most important things. If companies did not agree with that, "it was the problem of the companies." That attitude is dramatically, and increasingly, changing in Germany now. We are now talking about technical universities. Universities are looking carefully at companies and their current and potential employees. Universities have formed close relationships toward identifying both existing and future needs and bringing those needs into their curricula. But that is just one group of college graduates which is necessary for future competitiveness.

Just as important are apprentices. Companies require combinations of many qualified groups. The combination must be well integrated and harmonious. On all levels we need qualified people. Digitization has dramatically pushed forward these needs. Why? Because times when the supervisor knew the answer better than the employee are gone. You have a 26-year-old employee, and the boss is 42 years old—and your team is a problem.

In early German industry "the industry master" was the individual who told the people on the assembly line, "You made this mistake again; now look at this and do it that way." That approach will disappear. Qualified young people can be college trained or community college trained. Maybe employers like community college graduates even better because they have better practical backgrounds than those coming from the university with a bachelor's degree.

A further skill we have to learn is to see things from the customer's perspective. That is one aspect I would like to elucidate. If we talk about German industry, companies have to go through much data and research about their knowledge of customer demand, customer reactions, and customer needs to achieve better performance. I have visited SEW Diagnostics, Inc., headquartered in Gaffney, South Carolina, which produces electric motors. The company installed a manufacturing plant of the future highly integrated with digital components. This plant has a reduced cycle time to order an electro-motor part manufactured and shipped the next day in Germany. New thinking is coming up in that field, and nobody quite knows what it looks like because the data will change everything.

I'm fully convinced that we cannot say that change will come from the academic field or from those people trained from the universities if we don't release the innovation potential of community-trained people. Without that we will lose because the innovation process will become a complex analytical procedure. Everybody has to be part of innovation. We cannot distinguish anymore by academic degrees only. Everybody on his or her job must be empowered to innovate.

CHANGES IN BUSINESS DEMAND WILL DRIVE CURRICULUM CHANGE

You asked, "What will influence the curriculum of the future?" In my opinion, it will be company demand. The need for change in companies will drive curricula. We have 79 Chambers like mine all over Germany developing joint courses for different metal, IT, and electronics curricula.

We took industry-recognized certification and broke it down by competency. We said that in every class in the technical field we must give the student at least one certification. If the student leaves early, he or she is still carrying away something of value to the workplace. Students do not only get the three-hour credit for that class but at least one certification they can use in their workplace.

HOW NEW SKILLS ARE ADDED TO APPRENTICESHIPS

The apprenticeship system in Germany is organized like this: students spend half-time in the company and half-time in school. These are like community colleges. But in Germany, these are government training schools organized and financed by the state government. The apprentices get trained in the company by their trainers, but this is in-house training in the company. The person in the company is not a teacher but a master. Masters have been involved in their professions for many years. They are proud of doing this work for the company, and these masters know that it is up to them to make the best out of the young women or men they train. The second part of this training is performed by teachers. Many teachers have a business background as it pertains to the apprenticeship.

The masters drive change. Our students will not drop out. Our students in Germany will finish their three years. And then they graduate. They pass examinations at the end of their two to three-and-a-half years depending on the profession being trained. It is our job to design this examination. This examination comprises practical and theoretical components and is standard-ized nationally. The examiners are chosen, trained, and organized by the Chambers of Industry and Commerce. They are all masters from the hosting companies or the training schools.

The examiners do not earn salary for this examination requirement. They are volunteers. All over Germany, approximately 200,000 examiners are committed. People are doing this voluntarily, acting as examiners to train people. They get about $10 an hour for expenditures. It is a commitment to the economy to ensure sufficient professionals for the future. The company masters continue looking after their apprentices after they finish their profes-sional training. They also assess the graduates for additional skill training. That is crucial. Shortly before finishing their training period under their responsibility, they train them and coach them to be able to pass the test to become a professional. They are taught soft skills and hard skills. The mas-ters discuss these topics with their students.

Many apprentice degree holders succeed also for their families. A lot of them earn more money than those university bachelor's degree holders. Un-fortunately, there is a tendency for parents in Germany to think that their children are better-off if they go off to university. So this misconception is a big future challenge to the German industry that CCI does address. The Chamber is about to start a big program advising parents to consider their children attending a university or college but also to encourage their children to participate in one company's apprenticeship program and get a company apprenticeship degree.

It is a paid education. Attendees do not pay for tuition in these company apprenticeship programs. The student participants learn and earn as a company apprenticeship. They earn appropriate task and profession being learned. They become part of the company community. An employer in a three- or four-hundred-employee company will have on average three to five apprentices. After the training period, the student apprentice knows almost everyone in the company. If the student apprentice is a good performer, at least two to three employees will show up at the HR office to give recommendations and inform the company officials they would like the student apprentice to remain with the company.

I still owe you the second part of my answer about the curriculum. Today we are experiencing tremendous challenges because of fast-paced changes in skill demands. If we have a young person in a company apprenticeship training program, and he or she earns a certificate, it's enough for you to know that this student has acquired basic job skills. Still, that does not mean the student is qualified for the future. Assuming that was a feature of the old world. It is also wrong to assume that a single training program qualifies people to work for the rest of their lives. That thinking is obsolete. We continuously have to monitor what companies need.

Companies must get people workplace-ready and fit for work during the years of training on the job. But apprenticeship is only part A. Part B is about keeping people workplace-ready for additional learning for the Internet-based changes affecting business. Is the person flexible enough, and is the person adaptive enough? Does the person have the soft skills to fit in with the team and group process? The professional training gets the person ready in part A to start in real life. Real life is about change, change, change! Challenge, challenge, and challenge! Companies want this continuing learning experience from us.

People need to be ready to accept additional training. We do not want them to believe that they are finished because they have gone to school, passed the exam, earned a certificate or earned a degree. The apprenticeship is a unique way to prepare students for the workplace but also to train their personal trades. Workplace skills are part of the whole. We not only have to train but also must help to develop. The community college in Germany and the U.S. is an excellent place to lay the groundwork to prepare students not only with the workplace skills they need but also adjust their personal trades for the workplace.

Training never ends! But please, allow me to pose you a question. When does training begin?

Part IV

The Future

Part IV offers parting words about the future role of community colleges in workforce development.

Chapter Seventeen

Observations about Community Colleges

As we conducted interviews with so many community college leaders, hand-picked for their excellence, we heard a continuing refrain: "Professors, how well are we doing?" It is understandable that we heard that question, since we asked them for their thoughts in interviews but gave them few of our own.

Before answering that, we should make three observations that provide a background. First, higher education in the United States is undergoing a revolution. Second, government policy makers have consistently asked community colleges to be the front-line provider of employee training—either for prequalification (necessary for workers to find employment) or for continued employment (necessary for employment as times, and technologies, change). And third, community colleges are tasked to carry out their mission in educating and training while being asked to meet a growing number of government-imposed mandates. All three of these issues affect how we will answer the question posed by this volume's contributors.

THE REVOLUTION IN HIGHER EDUCATION

Many parents, children, and government leaders have not noticed the quiet revolution in higher education. Brick-and-mortar campuses are slowly being replaced by blended and virtual educational formats. In recent years, online education has increased at the expense of residential education. While online education has its challenges—high dropout rates among them—it continues to grow dramatically (Smith, 2015). Online education works well to transmit information but may need to be paired with on-site, hands-on experiences to build practical skills or encourage development of interpersonal skills.

At the same time, tenured faculty at research institutions are slowly being replaced by fixed-term and adjunct faculty, typically experienced practitioners. If large research-based schools are affected by these trends, driven by reductions in government funding of education and research, the trends also influence community colleges.

THE ROLE OF COMMUNITY COLLEGES

Government policy makers have traditionally regarded community colleges as a front-line provider of worker training. That is commendable and is one appropriate role that community colleges are well equipped to play. But community colleges could do so much more if they only had visionary government leaders to support them financially and politically. Community colleges are ideally positioned within local communities to provide the following services if they had increased funding and resources:

- Local labor forecasting
- Individual career counseling for students and alumni
- Employment exchanges for qualified workers and alumni
- Rapid responses to changes in local labor-force needs
- Long-term local community development efforts
- Long-term local economic development efforts
- Advice and counseling to small businesses and entrepreneurs
- Focal point for local innovation
- Focal point for consulting and outreach

While community colleges have historically provided some services in these areas, they have not been the central focus for such efforts, nor have they received adequate funding to increase the robust quality of the services they could provide. America's community colleges form a network of local—and "local" is the key word—educational institutions to be envied by other developed and developing economies and could play a much broader role. Let's spend some time to examine each of the bulleted points above.

Local Labor Forecasting

The U.S. government—and many state governments—conduct labor forecasting to predict changes in occupational demand. But improvements can be made in how well those forecasts are communicated to, and interpreted by, community college leaders and business leaders in the service areas of community colleges. There should be at least an annual process by which general labor forecasts are interpreted and communicated at the local level. Community colleges are well positioned to take the lead to do that and then focus community attention on areas of local occupational demand and changes in that demand.

Individual Career Counseling for Students and Alumni

Individual career counseling, sometimes called vocational guidance, could stand much improvement in many educational institutions—including secondary educational institutions and community colleges. Many resources are wasted as young adults, and even midcareer or late-career adults, struggle to determine and sustain career direction. If education is important for providing qualifications necessary for occupational entry, upskilling, and advancement, then education should be paired with career counseling so that students can make informed decisions about their education.

The need is all the more compelling because some research shows that 47 percent of college graduates get their first jobs in areas unrelated to their college majors, and 10 percent of enrolled college students admit that they do not want to work in areas related to their college majors (Phillips, 2014). With better, and continuing, career counseling, students would be better positioned to make more informed decisions based on their occupational interests and labor demand.

For some, career counseling is associated with "placement testing." But placement tests do not provide the basis for *continuing counseling* about educational choices and how those choices may relate to career success. Students and workers need more than superficial discussions or services about careers at community college entry or near graduation.

Employment Exchanges for Qualified Workers and Alumni

Community colleges are "suppliers" of labor. They can be a focal point for employers and employees to meet. Students tend to associate placement services with the help they need at or near graduation. But that relationship can, and should be, ongoing. Online methods make it easy for employers, students, and college alumni to communicate over time. In the future, such discussions may occur over extended time spans.

Rapid Responses to Changes in Local Labor-Force Needs

Time has become a critical resource. Community colleges should recognize that and establish methods by which to marshal their expertise quickly to respond to local labor market changes—such as plant closures, plant openings, downsizings by major employers, and sweeping regulatory changes.

It is a lesson the military has learned. That is why the armed services have rapid deployment forces, so that they have a group of highly trained people ready to respond to crisis at a moment's notice. It is a lesson health care has learned. That is why hospitals have rapid response teams to deal with medical emergencies and "triage" staff to determine what medical needs exist and match the resources to address them quickly. Community colleges should be organized to do the same for dramatic changes in labor market conditions affecting their service areas.

Long-Term Local Community Development Efforts

The notion of social capital has shown that relationships can have economic value (Putnam, 2001). Communities that have positive reputations tend to attract more employers, more people, and better opportunities. The reverse is also true: communities with reputations for crime and drug abuse tend to scare off prospective employers, citizens, and opportunities.

Community colleges play a major role in establishing a positive reputation, a "brand identity," for a community. They can be a focal point for organizing community development efforts and serve as a catalyst to "bring people together" to build a community's positive reputation. That role will likely grow more important in the future.

Long-Term Local Economic Development Efforts

Too often, local economic development and local workforce development professionals, including workforce investment boards, do not talk to each other (Crouch, 2003). Poor communication leads to wasted, and even conflicting, use of resources. Community colleges can and should play a major role as a focal point to bring together economic development professionals, workforce development professionals, community leaders, community college leaders, representatives from local educational institutions, and other stakeholder groups. By doing that, community colleges can facilitate more coordinated efforts among all key groups in communities.

Advice and Counseling to Small Businesses and Entrepreneurs

For many years, the Small Business Administration has offered consulting services through Small Business Development Centers to businesspeople who want to found, expand, or improve small businesses. Other groups, such as SCORE (Service Corps of Retired Executives), also offer services to small business owners. Small Business Development Centers are often already positioned on university campuses. But an excellent placement for them would be on community college campuses so that it is possible for business leaders to get local services easily—and in a centralized location.

Focal Point for Local Innovation

Community colleges are ideally positioned in local communities to be a focal point for local innovation and local business development. As a result, they should be encouraged to foster business incubators, business accelerators, and regional economic development groups. That notion can pair efforts to encourage business growth with the workforce development efforts that can support that business growth.

Focal Point for Consulting and Outreach

Although government leaders may associate community colleges with training centers, they can be—and do—so much more. Faculty can offer on-the-spot consulting services to community-based organizations. The institution can be a center for skill upgrading and sources of new knowledge as a locus for the diffusion of innovation. Those roles will, and should, grow more valuable in the future.

MANAGING GOVERNMENT MANDATES

Unfortunately, one challenge to overcome in meeting a broader mission is the burgeoning number of funded, and often unfunded, mandates with which community colleges are increasingly asked to comply. If any readers doubt that, consider the list of regulatory requirements for colleges and universities found at http://www.higheredcompliance.org/matrix/. While each law, rule, or regulation may make sense to taxpayers and government policy makers in isolation, the collective impact of them is to distract community college leaders from carrying out their mission, focusing instead on compliance issues. The sheer number of them cries out for process improvement and simplification.

Policies also have unintended consequences. For example, efforts to address child abuse prompted government policy makers to require teachers at educational institutions to undergo rigorous background checks. While those checks make good sense in theory, they often require educators to list every person with whom they have resided for decades in the past. Since few people are eager to have their private romantic relationships enter government databases for constant public scrutiny, many otherwise qualified teachers and instructors are discouraged from entering the teaching profession at any academic level. That problem affects community colleges in the same way that it affects major research institutions and public schools. It may, in part, explain the alarmingly precipitous drop in people willing to pursue teaching careers.

That is but one example. Many other examples of regulatory impacts may be cited that affect the performance of educational institutions generally and community colleges specifically.

So, back to the original issue. How would we grade community colleges? The answer is that we, the editors, would give community colleges a grade of A for carrying out their missions against the backdrop of the challenges facing them. But compared to the potential that these institutions have for doing more if they were adequately funded and if government leaders were more cognizant of what they are capable of, we would give them a grade of I (for Incomplete).

An important question is whether community colleges of the future will effectively transition to something greater as more classroom-based education and training moves to blended and virtual formats. If they do, it will lead to a new Golden Age in community-based education and training. If they do not, the continued long-term survival of community colleges may be in doubt.

One critical area for improvement is the community college's ability to respond quickly and efficiently in real time to meet the demands of our businesses, communities, and economic development agencies. When community colleges perfect their response time or "speed to market," then the concept of being a leader in providing workforce solutions, then they can achieve a long-term, sustainable competitive edge for community colleges.

The future professional development of community college workforce developers—as well as all community college staff who have a role to play in workforce development—will be an imperative for community colleges to keep pace with the rapid rate of change. We believe that this need will be met by the creation of a "National Workforce Development Academy for Community Colleges" that will provide entry-level to advanced training. Community college workforce developers will then be able to develop competencies in workforce development.

SUMMARY

Community college workforce developers must have an external presence visiting business, industry, government, and economic development groups to discuss workforce development and the benefits that the community college can bring to the table. The goal should be to establish partnerships that put the community college as an essential partner in workforce development. Community colleges need to be proactive and be willing to help and work together to better the communities of which they are a part.

Presidents, vice presidents, deans, and directors must be willing to interface directly with those they serve. The community college workforce developer also should be prepared to accept challenges to do new things. For example, when the announcement is made that a new industry is moving into a region, the workforce developer should be among the first to meet with them. If there is a plant closing, the workforce developer should be among the first to offer to meet with the employees to provide training and education to assist displaced workers to find new jobs. As community colleges have always done, they need to continue to train entry-level employees and upskill the existing workforce. It takes a community college team to accomplish these partnerships with government and economic development and workforce boards to assist with local workforce challenges.

REFERENCES

Crouch, E. (2003). *A rural perspective: A study of the utilization of workforce development in selected small businesses in Huntingdon County, Pennsylvania in 2002.* Unpublished Ph.D. dissertation. University Park: The Pennsylvania State University.

Phillips, C. (2014, November 16). A matter of degree: Many college grads never work in their major. *Times Free Press.* See: http://www.timesfreepress.com/news/life/entertainment/story/2014/nov/16/matter-degree-many-college-grads-never-work-/273665/.

Putnam, R. (2001). *Bowling alone: The collapse and revival of American community.* New York: Simon & Shuster.

Smith, A. (2015, April 21). The increasingly digital community college. *Inside Higher Ed.* See: https://www.insidehighered.com/news/2015/04/21/survey-shows-participation-online-courses-growing.

Chapter Eighteen

Final Words

There is an amazing convergence of opinions among community college leaders about issues of importance, as seen from the interviews in this volume. But the dialogue must continue as new leaders enter and old leaders leave.

Use this worksheet to guide future leader retreats and discussions in your community colleges:

	Questions	Answers
1	How would you define workforce development?	
2	What role do you believe that your community college should play in workforce development?	
3	What role do you believe that your community college should play in community development? Economic development? Individual career counseling? Training? Are there other roles that community colleges should play in workforce development they are not playing now?	
4	What barriers or challenges do you see in community colleges in carrying out their roles now? In the future?	
5	Technology is changing the face of education. Many senior institutions are moving their curricula to online formats. How do you see technology affecting community colleges?	
6	What role should the community college president play in workforce development? Can you clarify what Presidents should do and why you believe they should do that?	
7	What role should community college deans play in workforce development? Can you clarify what they should do and why you believe they should do that?	

8	What role should the community college faculty members play in workforce development? Can you clarify what faculty members should do and why you believe they should do that?	
9	What role should the community college workforce development leaders and staff play in workforce development? Can you clarify what workforce development staff members are doing well today? How could they improve?	
10	What role should the community college workforce development leaders and staff play in workforce development? Can you clarify what workforce development staff members are doing well today? How could they improve?	
11	What can or should community leaders do to better support community colleges?	
12	What trends do you foresee affecting community colleges or the workforce that might affect the ability of community colleges to meet the needs of future students? Imagine that you visited a community college 10 years from now. What would it look like? How would things be the same or different than they are today?	
13	Imagine that you were having a conversation with business leaders from your community about the role of community colleges. What would you tell them about that role?	

Index

About the Authors and Interviewees

William J. Rothwell, Ph.D., SPHR, SHRM-SCP, CPLP Fellow, is the President of Rothwell & Associates, Inc., and Rothwell & Associates, LLC (seewww.rothwellandassociates.com). He is also a Professor-in-Charge of the Workforce Education and Development program, Department of Learning and Performance Systems, at the Pennsylvania State University, University Park campus. He has authored, co-authored, edited, or co-edited 300 books, book chapters, and articles—including over 90 books.

Before arriving at Penn State in 1993, he had 20 years of work experience as a Training Director for Human Resources and Organizational Development in government and in business. He has also worked as a consultant for over 40 multinational corporations, including Motorola China, General Motors, Ford, and many others. In 2012 he earned the American Society for Training and Development's (ASTD) prestigious Distinguished Contribution to Workplace Learning and Performance Award, and in 2013 ASTD honored him by naming him a Certified Professional in Learning and Performance (CPLP) Fellow. In 2014 he was given the Asia-Pacific International Personality Brandlaureate Award (seehttp://www.thebrandlaureate.com/awards/ibp_bpa.php). He was the first U.S. citizen named a Certified Training and Development Professional (CTDP) by the Canadian Society for Training and Development in 2004.

His recent books include *Organization Development in Practice* (2016), *Mastering the Instructional Design Process*, 5th edition (2016), *Effective Succession Planning*, 5th edition (2015), *Practicing Organization Development*, 4th edition (2015), *The Leader's Daily Role in Talent Management* (2015), *Beyond Training and Development*, 3rd edition (2015), *Career Planning and Succession Management*, 2nd edition (2015), *Organization Development Fundamentals: Managing Strategic Change* (2015), *The Competency*

Toolkit (two volumes), 2nd edition (2015), *Creating Engaged Employees: It's Worth the Investment* (2014), *Optimizing Talent in the Federal Workforce* (2014), *Performance Consulting* (2014), the *ASTD Competency Study: The Training and Development Profession Redefined* (2013), *Becoming an Effective Mentoring Leader: Proven Strategies for Building Excellence in Your Organization* (2013), *Talent Management: A Step-by-Step Action-Oriented Approach Based on Best Practice* (2012), the edited three-volume *Encyclopedia of Human Resource Management* (2012), *Lean but Agile: Rethink Workforce Planning and Gain a True Competitive Advantage* (2012), *Invaluable Knowledge: Securing Your Company's Technical Expertise—Recruiting and Retaining Top Talent, Transferring Technical Knowledge, Engaging High Performers* (2011), *Competency-Based Training Basics* (2010), *Effective Succession Planning: Ensuring Leadership Continuity and Building Talent from Within*, 4th edition (2010), *Practicing Organization Development*, 3rd edition (2009), *Basics of Adult Learning* (2009), *HR Transformation* (2008), *Working Longer: New Strategies for Managing, Training, and Retaining Older Employees* (2008), and *Cases in Government Succession Planning: Action-Oriented Strategies for Public-Sector Human Capital Management, Workforce Planning, Succession Planning, and Talent Management* (2008). He can be reached by email at wjr9@psu.edu and by phone at 814-863-2581. He is at 310B Keller Building, University Park, PA, 16803.

Patrick E. Gerity, Ph.D., is the Vice President of Continuing Education, Workforce, and Community Development at Westmoreland County Community College (2006–present). He holds a BS, MS, and Ph.D. from the Pennsylvania State University. The Ph.D. was awarded in the area of workforce education and development. Dr. Gerity's dissertation, *A Study to Identify Community College Workforce Training and Development Professionals' Perceived Competencies and Perceived Professional Development Needs*, was endorsed by the American Association of Community Colleges (AACC) and the National Council for Continuing Education and Training (NCCET).

Dr. Gerity's career in workforce and economic development extends over a 30-year period during which he has developed, implemented, directed, and evaluated workforce, economic, and community development initiatives at WCCC, Community College of Allegheny County, Slippery Rock University of Pennsylvania, and the Office of the Chancellor of the Pennsylvania State System of Higher Education. Dr. Gerity is a Charter Member of AACC's Workforce Development Institute and was selected as the first AACC/US-DOL representative for Pennsylvania, serving from 1995 to 2004.

In 1998, Dr. Gerity was the Team Leader in the development of the Workforce and Economic Development Network of Pennsylvania (WEDnet-PA), which is in its 17th year and is the number-one state-funded training program for business and industry in the state. WEDnetPA's membership includes all 14 of the Pennsylvania community colleges and 13 other higher education institutions. Dr. Gerity was also the Team Leader in the development of ShaleNET, a nationally recognized job training program for entry-level employees for the natural gas industry funded by a USDOL–ETA Community-Based Job Training Grant (2010–2013), which trained and placed over 3,000 people in jobs in Pennsylvania, Ohio, West Virginia, and New York.

Dr. Gerity has served on the following boards: National Council for Workforce Education, National Council for Continuing Education and Training, and Catalyst Connection (MEP–Pittsburgh.) Dr. Gerity was also appointed for a three-year term to the AACC Commission for Workforce and Economic Development (1996–1998). He has been actively involved in Pennsylvania Workforce and Economic Development advisory groups from 1990 to the present. He has also had the privilege to meet with Secretary of Labor Hilda Solis, Assistant Secretary of Labor for the Employment and Training Administration Jane Oates, and Secretary of Energy Dr. Ernest Moniz to discuss the ShaleNET education and training program.

Dr. Gerity is a co-editor of two community college books along with Dr. William J. Rothwell, Penn State, and Elaine Gaertner, California Community College System: *Linking Training to Performance: A Guide for Workforce Development Professionals* (2004) and *Cases in Linking Workforce Development to Economic Development: Community College Partnering for Training, Individual Career Planning, and Community and Economic Development* (2008). Dr. Gerity has made presentations at the AACC Annual Convention, the AACC Workforce Development Institute, the National Council for Workforce Education, the National Council for Continuing Education and Training, and the League for Innovation.

Vernon L. Carraway, Ph.D., is the Chief Executive Officer of the Langston Du Bois Institute (LDI), a comprehensive and innovative human performance enhancement firm. As an educator and workforce learning performance professional, his area of expertise commences at the "Breakeven Point"—the position at which new leaders have added as much value to their new organization as they have consumed from it.

Dr. Carraway completed a BA with a concentration in sociology and psychology at Slippery Rock University of Pennsylvania, and went on to earn his Ed.M. at the University of Miami, Coral Gables, Florida. He completed his doctorate at the Pennsylvania State University, College of Education, Workforce Education and Development, University Park, Pennsylvania.

* * *

Dr. Bryan Albrecht has served as the President of Gateway Technical College since 2006. Serving as the college's chief executive, Dr. Albrecht oversees the college's 65 academic programs, 15 educational facilities, and a comprehensive $160 million budget and a progressive $4 million college foundation. Gateway represents Kenosha, Racine, and Walworth Counties and has an economic impact of more than $400 million annually. In this role, Dr. Albrecht represents the college on over 50 local, state, and national boards. He supports a comprehensive and vision-driven college, by increasing student support, contemporary programming, positive community partnerships, and innovative classrooms and facilities that reflect the business and industry. Guiding this vision is a team of over 600 education professionals and 400 industry advisory committee partners. Under Dr. Albrecht's leadership, Gateway has been recognized as a military-friendly college, an innovative college by the United States Department of Labor, a leadership college by the Association for Career and Technical Education, and a model college by the American Association of Community Colleges for sustainable education and economic development. Dr. Albrecht holds his BS, MS, and Ed.S. from the University of Wisconsin–Stout and his Ed.D. from the University of Minnesota.

Dr. Chris Bustamante serves as the President of Rio Salado College, the largest of the 10 Maricopa Community Colleges in Tempe, Arizona. Rio Salado serves nearly 59,000 students annually with more than 30,000 students online. Dr. Bustamante is a well-known advocate for increasing access to higher education and degree completion, and for forging transformational partnerships with business, government, and other educational providers. Besides his responsibilities at Rio Salado, Dr. Bustamante serves as the President for both the Continuous Quality Improvement Network and the National Community College Hispanic Council, and is the incoming Chair for the Council for Adult and Experiential Learning Board of Trustees. In addition, he serves on the American Association of Community Colleges Executive Committee, the Western Interstate Commission for Higher Education, and the National Council for State Authorization Reciprocity Agreements, and he chairs the American Council on Education's Center for Education Attainment and Innovation.

Deborah Davidson serves as the Vice President of Business and Workforce Solutions at Gateway Technical College in Kenosha, Wisconsin, where she oversees five advanced technology centers focused on transportation, engineering and manufacturing, information technology, health and emergency responder occupations, and a dual-enrollment high school academy. She is additionally responsible for outreach to business and industry, apprenticeship, customized training, business partnerships, and Gateway's successful

Boot Camp training programs. She has over 20 years' experience in higher education and is a past President of the National Coalition of Advanced Technology Centers. She also serves as the Director of Development on the Board of the National Coalition of Certification Centers. Davidson holds a bachelor's degree in management and communication from Concordia University Wisconsin and a master's degree in adult education from National Louis University in Evanston, Illinois. She has been with Gateway Technical College since 2001.

Mabel Edmonds is the Special Assistant to the President at Clover Park Technical College. She is an experienced leader in the fields of state government, workforce development, and postsecondary and K–12 education, which includes a distinguished 33-year tenure with the Saint Louis Public School District, leadership of multiple national and federally funded initiatives, and service on the Board of Directors as President for the National Council for Workforce Education. Her programs at Clover Park Technical College have received state and national awards for their success in helping low-income adults find employment. Prior to her current role, Edmonds was the Dean of Instruction for Aerospace, Technology, Manufacturing, and Workforce Development. As a former Policy Analyst for the Washington State Legislature House of Representatives, she has researched and reported on emerging issues and trends in education for state lawmakers. Edmonds earned her bachelor's degree at Harris Teachers College and her master's degree at the University of Missouri. She received additional leadership training and certification as a Reading Specialist.

Dr. Kenneth Ender is the President of William Rainey Harper College, a large community college located outside of Chicago, Illinois. Through partnerships and alliances, Dr. Ender has positioned Harper as a leading 21st-century community college by increasing graduation, transfer, and certificate completion rates; aligning Harper's curriculum with high schools; training students for new economy jobs; and implementing new accountability and transparency standards. Since he came to the college in 2009, Harper has experienced record graduation rates and a dramatic increase in the number of students who come to Harper college-ready. The college has also formed new alliances with businesses to address the shortage of skilled workers in key industries. Before coming to Harper, Dr. Ender served as the President of Cumberland County College in New Jersey for 11 years.

Dr. Larry A. Ferguson is the President of Bevill State Community College in Sumiton, Alabama. Prior to this appointment, Dr. Ferguson served as the Vice Chancellor of Economic Development and Workforce Solutions and Interim Vice Chancellor of Academic Affairs for the Kentucky Community and Technical College System (KCTCS). He has over 20 years of postsecondary education experience in the private sector and higher education. He has been engaged in career and technical education and workforce pipeline development for multiple industry sectors and was the primary KCTCS point of contact for global, national, and regional companies seeking workforce development solutions in Kentucky. Dr. Ferguson has also held positions at Ashland Community and Technical College in Ashland, Kentucky, where he served as an instructor, Dean of Community Workforce and Economic Development, and Dean of Resource Development and External Affairs. Prior to his positions in the community college arena, he held administrative positions in the private sector with ClientLogic, King's Daughters Medical Center, and Applied Card Systems. A product of Kentucky's community college system, Dr. Ferguson earned his bachelor's and master's degrees from Mountain State University in Beckley, West Virginia, and received his Ph.D. in educational leadership from Trident University in Cypress, California.

William H. Gary Sr. has served as the Executive Vice President of the Cuyahoga Community College (Tri-C) Workforce and Economic Development Division (WEDD) since July 2014. WEDD is the college's training arm, which prepares the workforce of tomorrow for jobs in fields such as manufacturing, information technology, health care, and public safety. Gary views Tri-C's role as critical to building a vibrant economy in Northeast Ohio. His background includes more than three decades of private and public sector management experience in a variety of fields. He came to Tri-C from Northern Virginia Community College, where he led economic development initiatives and oversaw job training programs.

Dr. Merrill Irving Jr. is a visionary leader with an accomplished record of serving diverse learning communities championing underserved and nontraditional students. As the fourth President of Hennepin Technical College's campuses in the suburban Minneapolis cities of Brooklyn Park and Eden Prairie, Minnesota, he leads the college in fulfilling its mission of providing excellence in career and technical education for employment and advancement. Dr. Irving's national roles include the American Association of Community Colleges, Learning Resource Network, National Council for Workforce Education, National Council on Black American Affairs, and National Council for Continuing Education and Training. He has received numerous awards, including the League for Innovation's Innovation of the Year Award in Biotechnology, Millennium Momentum Foundation Inc.'s Best and Brightest Fellowship at USC, and the Judith Herndon Fellowship to the West Virginia House of Delegates. Dr. Irving previously served as the Associate Vice President of Continuing Education, Training, and Workforce Development at Oakton Community College in Illinois, where he led strategic initiatives in workforce development, continuing education, lifelong learning, and academic collaborations with the school districts, local municipalities, and the workforce investment board. Prior to Oakton Community College, he was the Chairperson for Continuing Education and Professional Development at Miami Dade College, Wolfson Campus. Dr. Irving attended West Virginia University in Morgantown, earning his BA and MPA. He attained his doctorate in education psychology from the University of Southern California.

James Jacobs, Ph.D., is the President of Macomb Community College in Michigan and has over 40 years of experience in education. Prior to his appointment, he concurrently served as Director for the Center for Workforce Development and Policy at the college and as Associate Director for the Community College Research Center at Teachers College, Columbia University, where he now serves as a member of its board of directors. Jacobs earned his Ph.D. from Princeton University and specializes in the areas of workforce skills and technology, economic development, worker retraining, and community college workforce development. He is also a member of the Community College Advisory Panel to the Educational Testing Service in Princeton, New Jersey, and on the board of the Global Corporate College. Jacobs serves on several local boards, including the Center for Automotive Research, Metropolitan Affairs Council, Detroit Institute of Arts, United Way for Southeastern Michigan, and Advancing Macomb.

Professor Hans-Peter Mengele has been the Chief Executive Officer of the Chamber of Commerce and Industry (IHK) Karlsruhe, Germany, since 1998, and he heads the Technologiefabrik Karlsruhe (start-up center) and the IHK-Bildungszentrum Karlsruhe GmbH Germany (professional development training center). Prior to his appointment at the Chamber of Commerce, Prof. Mengele served as Chief of Staff to the Governor and as Head of the Department for International Policy to the State of Baden-Württemberg, Germany. The chamber provides innovative, structural, and international intelligence and services to its 64,000 members and holds responsibility for public administration in vocational education and training (VET). With 10,818 registered VET contracts in 2,448 companies, the chamber ensures a top-quality standard. Each year, 428 examining boards in vocational education and training and 58 examining boards in postsecondary training with a total of 2,500 voluntary examiners perform over 4,500 exams. In addition, 1,197 master examinations (occupational) have been processed, along with 989 occupational instructor qualification tests in 2015 alone. The IHK Karlsruhe initiated 756 agreements between 422 enterprises and 152 schools focusing on career and academic orientation activities and programs for students ready to leave school, getting prepared to make the significant decision. The IHK

Karlsruhe also reaches out to over 17,000 visitors annually with its start-a-career exposition. IHK Karlsruhe is cooperating with Central Piedmont Community College (CPCC), Charlotte, North Carolina, where Prof. Mengele is a member of the President's Council. The agreement with CPCC covers, among others, two official professional certificates in CNC and PLC issued in conjunction with the IHK Karlsruhe, Germany.

Dr. James Shemwell has been with the Arkansas Northeastern College since 1994, beginning his career as a satellite campus coordinator. He moved up the ranks at the college to become Dean for Technical Programs and Training in 1999, Vice President for Finance in 2010, and President in January 2013. From 1988 to 1994, he served as a Chief Financial Officer in the banking industry. Prior to that, Dr. Shemwell served as Assistant Director of the Small Business Development Centers at Arkansas State University and, later, Texas Tech University. Dr. Shemwell earned a bachelor's degree in accounting from Arkansas State University in 1985 and was named the university's "Top Graduate" by *Arkansas Business*. He later earned a master's degree in finance from Texas Tech and a doctoral degree in organizational leadership from the University of Phoenix. Dr. Shemwell is married to Dr. Bridget Shemwell, and has two grown sons.

Dr. Weiping Shi is the Director of the Institute of Vocational and Adult Education (IVAE) at East China Normal University. IVAE is dedicated to fostering vocational, adult master's, and Ph.D. degrees in the principle, curriculum, and teaching fields of vocational, technical, and adult education. Under Dr. Shi, IVAE has established Asian-wide fame in these fields, and is one of the best master's and doctoral centers for vocational, adult education in China.

Dr. Shi is committed to vocational education research and has to his credit over 20 national research programs, three UNESCO or British Council Joint Research Projects, 14 published books and monographs, and 159 articles in journals. He is also President of the Asian Academic Society of Vocational Education and Training, Vice Chairman of the China Vocational and Technical Education Society, and Chairman of the Academic Committee of the China Vocational and Technical Education Society.

Dr. Devin Stephenson is the President of Big Sandy Community and Technical College (BSCTC). A Sumiton, Alabama, native, Dr. Stephenson has nearly 40 years of experience in higher education. He served as President and CEO of Three Rivers College in Missouri prior to coming to BSCTC and has held several leadership positions within the Alabama Community College System, including Vice President of External Affairs and Dean of Students at Bevill State Community College, CEO of Snead State Community College, and Dean of Students at Walker State Technical College. Dr. Stephenson is a community college graduate. He earned an associate degree in science from Walker Junior College, followed by a bachelor of arts in business administration from Birmingham–Southern College and both master's and doctoral degrees in the administration of higher education from the University of Alabama. A member of the Southeast Kentucky Chamber of Commerce Board of Directors, Dr. Stephenson was named to the Commission on Leadership and Professional Development at the American Association of Community Colleges. Dr. Stephenson and his wife, Judy, reside in Paintsville. They have two adult children, Jon and JuliAnne.

Dr. John J. "Ski" Sygielski, Ed.D., became the seventh President of HACC, Central Pennsylvania's Community College, in July 2011. His previous appointments include President of Mount Hood Community College in Gresham, Oregon, and President of Lord Fairfax Community College in Middletown, Virginia. Dr. Sygielski is the past Chairman of the Board for the American Association of Community Colleges (AACC) and AACC's 21st-Century Commission on the Future of Community Colleges. He is a member of Harrisburg Rotary and serves on the boards of the Harrisburg Boys and Girls Club, Harrisburg Chamber of Commerce, and Pennsylvania's Workforce Investment Board. He earned his bachelor's degree in philosophy, two master's degrees in business and a doctorate in education, and an honorary associate degree. Dr. Sygielski and his husband, Steve Perrault, are residents of Harrisburg, Pennsylvania. A native of Cleveland, Ohio, Dr. Sygielski is the only member of his working-class family to have graduated from college.

Dr. Charles D. Terrell is the fourth President of Eastern West Virginia Community and Technical College (Eastern), bringing three decades of rural community college teaching and administrative experience. He is an advocate of building and strengthening relationships with business and industry employers by giving them direct input and involvement in developing workforce training programs delivered through a community college. "That way, the college stays in tune with the changing economic climate in the community and region," he pointed out, and "becomes and continues to be a valuable partner and contributor to economic development."

President Terrell signed the National Association for Community College Entrepreneurship Presidents for Entrepreneurship Pledge in 2011. Through the Presidents for Entrepreneurship Pledge, community college presidents commit to advance entrepreneurship in their communities and create an entrepreneurial culture on their campus and multiple access points to support local start-ups and small businesses. His goal is to ensure that Eastern is involved in one of the most pivotal conversations about what can be done to advance economic prosperity in the region. There are two reasons this is important:

1. Expanding entrepreneurship is vital to building a vibrant and sustainable economy.
2. Community colleges are ideally positioned to lead in furthering economic development and entrepreneurship based on accessibility, strong ties to local communities, affordability, and diversity of student populations.

Moving beyond the traditional role of workforce development, community colleges can advance local ecosystems by fostering an entrepreneurial mind-set and supporting entrepreneurs and job creation. In 2013 Eastern created the Institute for Rural Entrepreneurship and Economic Development to create, support, and sustain an innovation-based economy in the Potomac Highlands of West Virginia. "Higher education is not a sport—but as in sports," Dr. Terrell pointed out, "faculty, staff, students, and community are central players striving to reach specific goals. My goal is to be a good coach—inspiring, energizing, and facilitating the performance, learning, and development of every player. Because in our arena, when students and the community are successful," he emphasized, "the whole team wins."

Jen Worth serves as the Senior Vice President for Workforce and Economic Development for the American Association of Community Colleges (AACC). In this role, Worth oversees projects that partner community colleges with workforce boards, economic development entities, labor market intermediaries, and other community organizations to drive workforce and economic opportunity. Striving to make promising practices into common practices, she interfaces with federal agencies and fosters relationships with foundations and industry partners looking to align talent pipelines from colleges into growing employment sectors. In addition to the various projects in the department, Worth also directs the annual Workforce Development Institute and annual event for approximately 700 workforce development professionals at community colleges. She also staffs the Commission on Economic and Workforce Development and is the liaison for the following six AACC Affiliated Councils: Community Colleges of Appalachia, National Council for Continuing Education and Training, National Coalition of Advanced Technology Centers, National Council for Workforce Education, National Partnership for Environmental Technology Education, and Rural Community College Alliance. Worth has held positions at the National Center on Education and the Economy, the Academy for Educational Development, the Center for Post-Compulsory Education and Lifelong Learning, and the National Association of Workforce Boards. She serves on the board of SkillsUSA and the National Association for Community College Entrepreneurship. holds a master of public policy and management from the University Melbourne in Australia.

Dr. P. Anthony Zeiss holds a doctorate in community college administration from Nova University, a master's degree in speech (radio and television), and a bachelor's degree in speech education from Indiana State University. In 1992, Dr. Zeiss became the third President of Central Piedmont Community College in Charlotte, North Carolina. During his tenure, the college has grown from one campus to six and has become recognized as a national leader in workforce development. Dr. Zeiss has authored several books on economic development, adult literacy, national workforce development, and American history. Dr. Zeiss is a professional speaker and a frequent keynoter on college resource development, workforce development, leadership, and career development. Dr. Zeiss is past Chair of the Board of the American Association of Community Colleges and past Board Chair for the League for Innovation, and was the Association of Community College Trustees' National CEO of the year for 2004–2005.

161

She
of

Made in the USA
Middletown, DE
04 December 2017